Allan Shepard

Gods Ancestors
The Rescue of Celtic Rituals

Original Title: *Deuses Ancestrais - O Resgate dos Rituais Celtas*
Copyright © 2025, published by Luiz Antonio dos Santos ME.
This book is a non-fiction work that explores practices and concepts in the field of Celtic spirituality and ancestral wisdom. Through a comprehensive approach, the author provides practical tools for connecting with Celtic mythology, rituals, and philosophies that guide spiritual development and inner transformation.

1st Edition
Production Team
Author: Allan Shepard
Editor: Luiz Santos
Cover Design: Studios Booklas / Ethan Turner
Consultant: Richard Donovan
Researchers: Fiona Matthews, James O'Connell, Sarah Greene
Layout: Patrick Monroe
Translation: Julia Bennett
Publication & Identification
Gods Ancestors: The Rescue of Celtic Rituals
Published by: Booklas Publishing, 2025
Categories: Celtic Spirituality / Mythology & Religion
DDC: 299.16 / **CDU:** 133.4
All Rights Reserved To:
Luiz Antonio dos Santos ME / Booklas Publishing
No part of this book may be reproduced, stored in a retrieval system, or transmitted in any form—electronic, mechanical, photocopying, recording, or otherwise—without prior written permission from the copyright holder.

Summary

Sistematic Index 5
Prologue 11
Chapter 1 The Call of the Soul.. 13
Chapter 2 Embracing Divine Diversity..................................... 17
Chapter 3 The Celtic World 24
Chapter 4 Meeting the Celtic Gods.. 31
Chapter 5 Non-Physical Realities 38
Chapter 6 From the Irrational to the Divine............................. 45
Chapter 7 The Call to the Disciple... 53
Chapter 8 Dagda The Good God, the Father of All 59
Chapter 9 Morrigan The Goddess of War, Destiny and Sovereignty 67
Chapter 10 Lugh The Brilliant God, Master of Arts.................. 75
Chapter 11 Brigid The Triple Goddess of Fire, Healing, and Poetry 82
Chapter 12 Cernunnos God of Wild Nature............................. 89
Chapter 13 Danu The Mother Goddess, Source of Life 96
Chapter 14 Gods and Goddesses of Nature 104
Chapter 15 Spirits and Ancestors.. 112
Chapter 16 Understanding Celtic Rituals................................. 119
Chapter 17 Creating Sacred Space... 127
Chapter 18 Steps on the Sacred Journey 135
Chapter 19 Celtic Invocation and Prayers............................... 144
Chapter 20 Celtic Prayers Models and Inspiration 152
Chapter 21 Celtic Offerings to Gods and Spirits 160

Chapter 22 Tools of Power and Magic 169
Chapter 23 Introspection and Spiritual Connection 177
Chapter 24 The Continuing Journey 185
Chapter 25 Conduct and Responsibility................................... 194
Chapter 26 Next Steps on the Celtic Journey 203

Sistematic Index

Chapter 1: The Call of the Soul - Discusses the spiritual emptiness and unease prevalent in the modern world, highlighting the need for a deeper, more authentic spirituality.

Chapter 2: Embracing Divine Diversity - Explores the concept of divine diversity, challenging the idea of monotheism as the only valid form of spiritual expression and highlighting the richness and complexity of polytheistic traditions, particularly in the Celtic context.

Chapter 3: The Celtic World - Delves into the history, culture, and spiritual legacy of the Celtic peoples, emphasizing their deep connection to nature, their vibrant mythology, and their enduring influence on modern spirituality.

Chapter 4: Meeting the Celtic Gods - Introduces the reader to the vast and complex Celtic pantheon, exploring the archetypal energies, attributes, and interrelationships of the various gods and goddesses, and their continued relevance to contemporary spirituality.

Chapter 5: Non-Physical Realities - Discusses the Celtic concept of the Otherworld and the existence of non-physical dimensions, exploring their nature, inhabitants, and the importance of interaction with these subtle realms for spiritual growth and understanding.

Chapter 6: From the Irrational to the Divine - Examines the nature of consciousness, outlining a spectrum of consciousness from the irrational to the spiritual, and emphasizing the importance of expanding consciousness beyond the rational mind to connect with a deeper, more comprehensive reality.

Chapter 7: The Call to the Disciple - Explores the nature of the call to discipleship in the Celtic tradition, discussing the various forms it can take, the importance of sincere intention, and the initial steps to embark on a path of spiritual learning and devotion.

Chapter 8: Dagda - The Good God, the Father of All - Delves into the archetype of Dagda, the "Good God" and "Father of All" in the Celtic pantheon, exploring his attributes, symbols, domains, and the relevance of his energy for the modern disciple.

Chapter 9: Morrigan - The Goddess of War, Destiny, and Sovereignty - Examines the complex and multifaceted archetype of Morrigan, the Celtic goddess of war, destiny, and sovereignty, discussing her various aspects, symbols, and the transformative power she offers to those who seek her.

Chapter 10: Lugh - The Brilliant God, Master of Arts - Explores the archetype of Lugh, the "Shining One" and master of all arts in Celtic mythology, emphasizing his connection to light, knowledge, skill, and his inspiration for those seeking excellence and creative expression.

Chapter 11: Brigid - The Triple Goddess of Fire, Healing, and Poetry - Unveils the archetype of Brigid, the triple goddess of fire, healing, and poetry in Celtic tradition, discussing her three main aspects - Maiden, Mother, and Crone - and the relevance of her energy for healing, inspiration, and protection.

Chapter 12: Cernunnos - God of Wild Nature - Delves into the archetype of Cernunnos, the Celtic god of wild nature, animals, fertility, and abundance, emphasizing his connection to the untamed forces of the natural world and the importance of honoring and protecting nature.

Chapter 13: Danu - The Mother Goddess, Source of Life - Explores the archetype of Danu, the primordial Mother Goddess in Celtic mythology, source of all life, and divine ancestor of the Tuatha Dé Danann, emphasizing her connection to creation, fertility, nourishment, and maternal protection.

Chapter 14: Gods and Goddesses of Nature - Discusses the importance of nature deities in Celtic spirituality, exploring the various types of nature gods and goddesses, their domains, attributes, and the relevance of honoring and connecting with these divine forces for a harmonious life.

Chapter 15: Spirits and Ancestors - Delves into the realm of spirits and ancestors in Celtic cosmology, exploring the concept of the Sidhe (fairy folk), the importance of ancestral veneration, and the ethical considerations for interacting with these spiritual beings.

Chapter 16: Understanding Celtic Rituals - Provides a comprehensive overview of Celtic rituals, exploring their purposes, philosophy, key elements, and the importance of intention, reciprocity, and connection with the sacred in ritual practice.

Chapter 17: Creating Sacred Space - Guides the reader through the process of creating a sacred space for Celtic rituals, detailing the steps of purification, consecration, and casting the magic circle, emphasizing the importance of intention, symbolism, and energetic protection in ritual practice.

Chapter 18: Steps on the Sacred Journey - Outlines the basic structure of a Celtic ritual, detailing the seven main steps involved in the ritual process, from opening and purification to closing and grounding, highlighting the flexibility and adaptability of the ritual format to individual needs and intentions.

Chapter 19: Celtic Invocation and Prayers - Explores the significance of invocation and prayer in Celtic rituals, discussing their purpose, different forms, and the importance of language, intention, and emotional state in establishing communication with the sacred.

Chapter 20: Celtic Prayers - Models and Inspiration - Offers practical examples and models of Celtic invocations and prayers directed to various deities of the Celtic pantheon, providing inspiration and guidance for creating personalized devotional practices and deepening the connection with the sacred.

Chapter 21: Celtic Offerings to Gods and Spirits - Discusses the practice of offerings in Celtic rituals, exploring the philosophy behind offerings, the various types of offerings, and the importance of intention, reciprocity, and respect in honoring deities, spirits, and ancestors.

Chapter 22: Tools of Power and Magic - Delves into the world of Celtic ritual instruments, exploring their symbolism, purpose, and significance as extensions of the practitioner's will, highlighting the importance of consecration, proper use, and deep understanding of these magical tools.

Chapter 23: Introspection and Spiritual Connection - Examines the role of meditation and visualization in Celtic spirituality, discussing the various techniques and benefits of these practices for introspection, self-knowledge, spiritual connection, and expansion of consciousness.

Chapter 24: The Continuing Journey - Discusses the integration of Celtic spirituality into everyday life, offering practical ways to connect with nature, honor ancestors, cultivate devotion to deities, practice magic, and live in accordance with Celtic values and principles.

Chapter 25: Conduct and Responsibility - Explores the ethical dimension of Celtic spirituality, discussing the values and principles that guide the modern Celtic disciple, emphasizing the importance of honor, integrity, respect for nature, courage, wisdom, hospitality, and balance in personal and spiritual development.

Chapter 26: Next Steps on the Celtic Journey - Offers guidance and resources for those seeking to deepen their Celtic journey, including suggestions for further study, ritual practice, connecting with the Celtic community, exploring specific traditions, and integrating Celtic ethics into daily life.

Prologue

In an era marked by the incessant search for meaning and connection, a growing number of people have turned to ancient traditions in search of wisdom and guidance. Ancestral beliefs, with their deep connection to nature, the cycles of life, and reverence for the divine, offer a path for those yearning for a more authentic and rooted spirituality. In this context, Celtic spirituality, with its rich mythology, magical rituals, and profound reverence for nature, has sparked increasing interest worldwide.

"The Return of the Celtic Gods" is a guide for those who feel called to explore this ancestral path. With clear and engaging language, the author, Luiz Santos, invites us on a journey of rediscovery of Celtic wisdom, revealing the mysteries of the gods and goddesses, rituals and practices, and the philosophy that sustains this rich spiritual tradition.

This book is an invitation to immerse yourself in the magic of the Celtic world, to connect with ancestral energies, and to awaken the divine spark that resides within each of us. If you seek a more authentic spirituality, rooted in nature and the cycles of life, this book is an essential guide for your journey. May the reading of this book lead you to a deep connection with

Celtic wisdom and inspire you to walk your own path back to the sacred.
 Luiz Santos
 Editor

Chapter 1
The Call of the Soul

The modern world, with its technological wonders and promises of constant progress, has paradoxically left many of us feeling a deep void. Life, which should be filled with meaning and connection, often reveals itself as an arid journey, marked by a sense of disconnection and lack of genuine purpose. We observe the frenetic pace of daily life, the incessant pursuit of material possessions, the superficiality of social interactions mediated by screens, and we ask ourselves: is this all there is? There is, at the core of the contemporary human experience, a growing unease, a yearning for something more substantial, something that transcends the ephemeral nature of the material world and touches the deepest essence of our being.

We have been conditioned to believe that success is measured in numbers, that happiness lies in the possession of increasingly sophisticated objects and experiences, that our identity is built through external approval and validation on social media. We are bombarded by advertising messages that urge us to consume incessantly, filling time and space with acquisitions that, however, never manage to quench the soul's thirst. We work hard to accumulate wealth, often sacrificing our health, our relationships and our inner peace, in search of an illusory security that never fully materializes. This incessant pursuit of the material, although it occupies and distracts us, paradoxically distances us more and more from what really matters: the connection with ourselves, with others and with something greater that transcends us.

Modern society, in its incessant search for the rational and the scientific, has often neglected the deep spiritual needs that have always been part of the human experience. We have reduced the world to equations and numbers, seeking logical explanations for everything, and we have discarded as superstition or mere fantasy that which does not fit into our limited mental models. We have forgotten that the human being is not just a collection of cells and chemical reactions, but also a being endowed with emotions, intuition, imagination and an innate thirst for transcendence. By excessively valuing the tangible and the measurable, we lose the ability to perceive the subtleties of the invisible world, the subtle energies that permeate us and connect us to something greater.

Consumerism, that driving force of modern society, has promised us happiness through the acquisition of goods and services. We have been led to believe that the next purchase, the next gadget, the next consumer experience will be able to provide us with the lasting satisfaction that we so long for. However, reality proves to be implacable: the excitement of the purchase is ephemeral, the novelty quickly fades away, and we soon find ourselves back at the same starting point, with the same inner emptiness, desperately seeking the next dose of instant gratification. This vicious cycle of consumption imprisons us in a vicious circle, where the search for external happiness becomes a constant source of dissatisfaction and frustration.

In the midst of this modern disenchantment, many find themselves adrift, without a compass, lost in a sea of uncertainties and existential anxieties. The feeling of lack of purpose settles in, corroding the joy of living and obscuring the horizon with a fog of hopelessness. Life loses its brilliance, the colors fade, and the journey becomes a burden too heavy to bear. This "disease of the modern soul", as some call it, manifests itself in various ways: anxiety, depression, social isolation, addictions, self-destructive behaviors, and a deep sense of alienation in relation to oneself and the world.

However, in the midst of this darkness, lies also the seed of hope. The emptiness we feel, this unease that assails us, can be interpreted not as a sign of defeat, but as a call, an invitation to seek something deeper and more authentic. It is in the recognition of this spiritual need that lies the opportunity to begin a journey of rediscovery, of reconnection with the ancestral sources of wisdom that can guide us back to a path of meaning and fullness. The ancient spiritual traditions, with their deep understanding of human nature and the universe, offer us a map, a roadmap to follow this journey of healing and transformation. They remind us that true happiness is not found in the external world, but within ourselves, in connection with the sacred that resides in every human being and in all manifestations of life.

Ancestral spirituality, in its diverse forms and expressions, can fill this void that modernity has imposed on us. It invites us to look beyond the veil of material illusion, to awaken to the reality that we are spiritual beings living a human experience, and not the other way around. It offers us tools and practices to cultivate inner peace, connection with nature, respect for other beings, and the search for a greater purpose that transcends our individual existence. By reconnecting with the roots of ancestral wisdom, we can find the cure for the "disease of the modern soul", restoring the joy of living, the meaning of the journey and the deep connection with the mystery of existence. This book is an invitation to this rediscovery, a journey towards awakening to the Celtic gods, an ancestral path that still pulsates with the force of life and the promise of a reunion with the sacred.

Chapter 2
Embracing Divine Diversity

Here, on the threshold of a new cycle of reflections, we are invited to peer into the depths of the human soul, that vast and often unexplored territory. In times where the vertigo of modernity assails us, where material progress is presented as a universal panacea, paradoxically, a diffuse feeling of incompleteness emerges, a yearning for something that transcends the tangible. There is a subtle call, almost inaudible amidst the clamor of the world, an invitation to unravel what is hidden in the subtext of existence, in the shadows projected by the incessant search for external validation and fleeting achievements. It is in this liminal space, between the gleaming surface of the contemporary world and the unexplored depths of the spirit, that our journey begins.

This feeling of emptiness, this unease that permeates the contemporary human experience, does not arise from nothing. It is, to a large extent, a product of cultural constructs, of interpretative lenses that were tacitly imposed upon us and that shape our perception of reality at deep levels. From an early age, we are immersed in narratives that delimit the field of the possible, that establish boundaries between the visible and the invisible, the material and the spiritual. One of these narratives, particularly influential in Western contexts, circumscribes the divine to a single manifestation, to a singular entity that demands exclusivity and unconditional reverence. This perspective, while it may offer a sense of order and security to some, simultaneously, can act as a restrictive filter, obscuring the myriad of other ways in which the sacred can reveal itself.

It is imperative, therefore, to question the premises that underpin this singular view of the divine. Can the vastness of the spiritual universe, with its countless dimensions and manifestations, be truly contained within the limits of a single belief? The history of humanity, in its rich and multifaceted course, presents us with a diverse panorama of cultures that flourished under the aegis of plural belief systems, revering a multiplicity of forces and entities that personified the multiple aspects of life and nature. Exploring these other paths, opening ourselves to this diversity of perspectives, does not imply frontally rejecting one belief in favor of another, but rather expanding our horizon of understanding, recognizing that the search for the sacred can take on innumerable forms, all of them valid and enriching in their singularity.

It is crucial to question the idea that monotheism represents the only absolute truth, the only correct way to relate to the divine. The history of humanity reveals to us a myriad of cultures and civilizations that flourished under the aegis of polytheistic belief systems, venerating a diversity of gods and goddesses, each one personifying different aspects of nature, of life and of the human experience. Civilizations such as the Greek, the Roman, the Egyptian, the Hindu, among so many others, built profound and lasting cultural and spiritual legacies, based on the premise of divine multiplicity. This rich tapestry of polytheistic beliefs demonstrates that the worship of multiple gods is not an aberration or a primitive form of spirituality, but rather a valid and complex expression of the human search for the sacred.

The belief in a single God, often presented as superior and more evolved, can be seen, from another perspective, as a product of a certain historical and cultural context, and not as a universal and immutable truth. Monotheism, in its diverse forms, emerged at specific moments in history, shaped by political, social and cultural forces that influenced the way societies organized themselves and understood the world. By absolutizing a single form of belief, we run the risk of ignoring the richness and diversity of other spiritual traditions that have flourished throughout history, closing ourselves off to other equally valid and enriching perspectives.

Embracing divine diversity means opening the doors of our perception to the possibility that spiritual reality is multifaceted, complex and infinitely richer than we can conceive within the limits of a restricted monotheistic vision. It means recognizing that the divine manifests itself in innumerable forms, in different planes and dimensions, and that each divinity, each spirit, each force of nature, represents a unique and valuable facet of the whole. It is like contemplating an exuberant garden: beauty does not reside only in a single flower, but in the myriad of colors, shapes and perfumes that harmonize in a vibrant symphony. In the same way, the beauty of the spiritual universe resides in its diversity, in the multiplicity of divinities that inhabit it and animate it.

In the specific context of Celtic spirituality, polytheism manifests itself in a vibrant and poetic way. The ancient Celts venerated a rich and complex pantheon of gods and goddesses, the Tuatha Dé Danann, beings of power and beauty who personified the forces of nature, the aspects of the human psyche and the mysteries of existence. From Dagda, the good god and father of all, to Morrigan, the warrior and prophetic goddess, passing through Lugh, the solar god and master of the arts, and Brigid, the triple goddess of fire, of healing and of poetry, the Celtic pantheon offers a rich range of divinities for us to connect with and seek help and inspiration. Each of these gods and goddesses represents an archetype, a primordial force that resonates within us and that we can invoke to guide us on our personal journey.

By opening ourselves to the Celtic polytheistic perspective, we are not necessarily rejecting other forms of belief, but rather expanding our understanding of the divine. It is not a matter of replacing one belief system with another, but rather of enriching our worldview, recognizing that the sacred manifests itself in multiple ways and that different paths can lead us to the same primordial source. The beauty of polytheism lies precisely in its capacity to embrace diversity, to celebrate the multiplicity of divine expressions and to connect us with the sacred in a more personal and multifaceted way. Instead of limiting our devotion to a single distant and unattainable divinity, we can cultivate intimate and meaningful relationships with different gods and goddesses, seeking the specific help of each one in different aspects of our lives.

It is in this recognition of divine plurality that we find an invitation to the expansion of our own spirituality. Instead of restricting ourselves to a single interpretative lens of the sacred, we are encouraged to contemplate the spiritual universe as a vast and multifaceted garden, where countless flowers bloom in distinct colors, shapes and aromas. Each polytheistic tradition, with its unique pantheon of gods and goddesses, offers a singular path to the connection with the transcendent, revealing unexplored facets of the human psyche and the interconnected web of life. By opening ourselves to this diversity, we enrich our own spiritual journey, transcending the limitations of a singular vision and embracing the vastness of the divine mystery in its totality. This openness does not imply completely abandoning the roots of our own tradition, but rather cultivating a posture of humility and receptivity before the infinite complexity of the sacred, recognizing that spiritual truth is not restricted to a single dogma or system of beliefs, but manifests itself in myriads of forms, each one with its own intrinsic beauty and wisdom.

The intrinsic beauty of embracing divine diversity also lies in the possibility of establishing a more intimate and personal relationship with the sacred. In polytheism, the pantheon of gods and goddesses does not present itself as a distant and unattainable entity, but rather as a vibrant community of forces and archetypes with which we can cultivate meaningful relationships. Each divinity, with its unique personality and its specific domains, offers a particular point of contact with the divine, allowing us to seek help and inspiration in different aspects of our lives. Whether seeking the wisdom of a goddess of justice in moments of moral challenge, or invoking the creativity of a god of the arts to propel personal expression, polytheism invites us to weave a complex network of relationships with the sacred, where devotion becomes a multifaceted and enriching journey. This more relational and personalized approach to spirituality can bring a sense of closeness and intimacy with the divine, nurturing the soul and strengthening our connection with the primordial source of life.

Ultimately, the journey towards divine diversity is an invitation to the expansion of consciousness and the overcoming of limiting dogmas. By questioning the premises of exclusivist monotheism and opening ourselves to the richness of polytheism, we begin a process of deconstruction of mental and emotional barriers that imprison us to restricted worldviews. This expansion of perspective is not limited only to the field of spirituality, but reverberates in all dimensions of our existence, fostering tolerance, respect and appreciation for diversity in all its forms. By recognizing divine multiplicity, we learn to value the plurality of voices, cultures and experiences that enrich the fabric of human life, understanding that true unity does not reside in uniformity, but rather in the celebration of difference. May this reflection on divine diversity inspire us to follow a path of openness, questioning and expansion of consciousness, towards a more inclusive, vibrant and truly transforming spirituality.

Chapter 3
The Celtic World

In our incessant search to understand the vastness of the spiritual, we inevitably confront ourselves with the plurality of the divine. If once we were content with singular and limited visions, the expansion of consciousness impels us to question: Is the tapestry of human faith reduced to a single thread? When contemplating the myriads of cultures that flourished and declined throughout the eons, we perceive the emanation of countless belief systems, each a unique portal to the transcendent. This finding launches us on an exploratory journey, a yearning to unravel spiritual paradigms that reverberate with the complexity and diversity of existence itself. Where, then, can we find an ancestral echo of this multifaceted perception of the sacred, a system that unfolds in multiple divinities and invites us to a broader connection with the forces that shape the universe?

The answer to this question resides in ancient traditions, in cultural legacies that, despite the veil of time, still pulse with a vital energy. It is not about searching in modern dogmas or contemporary interpretations, but rather diving into the depths of human history, where entire civilizations have woven intricate networks of beliefs, rituals, and mythologies. These ancestral systems, often shrouded in mystery and transmitted through generations by oral and esoteric practices, offer us a rich and complex panorama of polytheism. They not only validate the multiplicity of the divine, but also give us concrete ways to establish a meaningful relationship with the sacred in its various manifestations. Amidst this vast ocean of ancestral wisdom, a particular legacy emerges, a world rich in symbolism and power that calls for our attention.

This legacy, immersed in millennial mists and yet vibrant in its essence, is the Celtic World. A universe of beliefs and practices that flourished in distant lands and remote times, but which still resonates with an inexplicable force in our present. As we approach this ancestral domain, we are invited to unravel the secrets of a spirituality deeply connected to nature, permeated by evocative myths and inhabited by a myriad of divinities. It is in this ancestral context, rich in history and meaning, that we find a remarkable example of a polytheistic belief system, a concrete way to explore the connection with the sacred in its multiple faces. Let us prepare, therefore, to enter the mysteries of the Celtic World, a journey that will lead us to rediscover the magic and power of a millennial spiritual tradition.

The Celtic peoples, with their rich and complex history, flourished in various regions of Europe during Antiquity and the Middle Ages, leaving a cultural legacy that resonates to this day. It was not a politically unified civilization, like the Roman Empire, but rather a set of peoples with interconnected languages, customs, and beliefs, sharing a common cultural identity. From the British Isles and Gaul (present-day France) to the Iberian Peninsula, Central Europe and even parts of Asia Minor, the Celtic influence extended over vast territories, shaping landscapes, cultures and imaginations.

Celtic spirituality, intrinsically linked to their culture, was deeply immersed in nature. The ancient Celts venerated the forces of nature as divine manifestations, perceiving the sacred in the ancestral trees, in the crystalline springs, in the imposing mountains and in the wild animals. They believed that the natural world was permeated by spirits and subtle energies, and that the connection with nature was fundamental to harmony and spiritual well-being. This deep reverence for nature was reflected in their rituals, their arts, their poetry and their social organization, creating a vibrant culture in balance with the world around them.

Exploring the Celtic world is diving into a universe of mystery and magic. Their myths and legends, transmitted orally by generations of bards and druids, populate the imaginary with brave heroes, powerful goddesses, fantastic creatures and mythical landscapes. Stories like that of the Arthurian Cycle, the Welsh Mabinogion, the Irish Ulster Cycle, among so many others, reveal a rich and complex worldview, where the human world and the divine world intertwine, where magic is a force present in everyday life, and where the spiritual journey is a constant adventure in search of wisdom and transformation.

Even after the fall of the ancient Celtic world in the face of Roman expansion and the rise of Christianity, the Celtic legacy did not disappear. It survives in modern Celtic languages (such as Irish, Scottish Gaelic, Welsh, Breton, Cornish and Manx), in folk traditions, in folklore, in music, in art and, most importantly, in spirituality which, although often dormant, continues to pulse beneath the surface of European culture and elsewhere in the world where the Celtic diaspora has settled. Today, we observe a growing interest in rescuing and revitalizing Celtic traditions, seeking in ancestral wisdom a guide for modern life.

Within Celtic culture, a particularly beautiful and relevant concept for our spiritual journey is that of "Anam Cara", which can be translated as "soul friend". This concept describes a deep and spiritual connection between two people, a friendship that transcends the superficial plane and reaches the deepest essence of being. In the Celtic tradition, the figure of the Anam Cara was highly valued, representing a companion on a spiritual journey, an intimate confidant who understood the soul in its totality, offering support, encouragement and challenge on the path of self-knowledge and evolution. This concept reminds us of the importance of genuine spiritual relationships in our journey, of the need to cultivate friendships that inspire us to grow, to become better versions of ourselves and to reconnect with the sacred.

The Celtic legacy, therefore, is not just a repository of fascinating myths and legends, but also a practical guide for modern life. Celtic values, such as honor, courage, creativity, loyalty, hospitality and, above all, deep respect for nature, resonate with the needs and yearnings of contemporary human beings. In an increasingly individualistic, materialistic and disconnected world from nature, ancestral Celtic wisdom offers us a powerful antidote, a path back to harmony, balance and fullness. By rescuing these values and principles, we can build a more meaningful, authentic and connected life with the sacred that surrounds us and resides within us.

The Celtic heritage, therefore, reveals itself to be much more than a mere set of ancient ruins or enchanting legends; it is configured as a compass for the contemporary soul. In a world that often impels us to fragmentation and superficiality, the Celtic worldview offers a deep invitation to integrality. By embracing the sacredness of nature, as the ancient Celts did, we are reminded of our interconnection with the fabric of life, of which we are an inseparable part. The veneration of trees, waters and mountains is not limited to mere ritualism, but rather a recognition that divinity manifests itself in every particle of the universe. This ancestral ecological perception resonates urgently in our time, urging us to rethink our relationship with the planet and to act as responsible guardians of the Earth. Celtic wisdom teaches us that the health of our spirit is intrinsically linked to the health of the natural world that welcomes us, and that the search for inner harmony must necessarily be reflected in an external harmony with the environment.

Furthermore, the appreciation of community and authentic relationships, personified in the concept of "Anam Cara", emerges as a beacon amidst the growing wave of individualism that plagues modern society. The search for deep connections, for friendships that nurture the soul and drive spiritual growth, proves essential for a full and meaningful journey. The Celtic tradition reminds us that we are not alone in our search for the sacred, and that the support, encouragement and challenge offered by a true "soul friend" are invaluable for our personal and spiritual development. Cultivating these genuine relationships, based on mutual understanding and deep respect, becomes an act of resistance against the superficiality and loneliness that often permeate contemporary life. By strengthening the bonds that unite us, we build more resilient and compassionate communities, capable of facing the challenges of the world with courage and hope.

Ultimately, the Celtic legacy invites us on a journey of rediscovery and revitalization of essential values for building a more humane and harmonious future. Honor, courage, creativity, loyalty, hospitality and, above all, a deep respect for nature, are configured as pillars for an authentic and connected life with the sacred. By integrating these principles into our daily lives, we can tread a path back to fullness, balance and harmony that we so yearn for. Ancestral Celtic wisdom is not restricted to a distant past, but rather pulses as a living source of inspiration and guidance for the present and for future generations. By opening ourselves to this millennial legacy, we allow the magic and power of the

Celtic World to continue to illuminate our path, guiding us towards a more hopeful and spiritually enriched future.

Chapter 4
Meeting the Celtic Gods

Here we are, on the edge of a realm that pulsates with the echoes of time immemorial, a domain where the veil between worlds becomes thin, and the whispers of antiquity resonate with unparalleled power. We have left behind the exploration of the Celtic cultural tapestry, with its threads of enigma and ancestral legacy that captivated us. Now, we are called to penetrate the very heart of its spiritual essence, to unravel the mysteries that emanate from its divine figures. Let us prepare for a deep immersion into the universe of the Celtic Gods, primordial entities whose stories and energies shaped the worldview of a people and continue to reverberate through the ages, influencing the very fabric of existence. This is an invitation to transcend the surface of history and legend, and connect with the archetypal forces that personify ancestral Celtic wisdom.

In this dive into the depths of the Celtic world, we are confronted with a divine constellation of impressive magnitude. This is not a static or monolithic pantheon, but rather a complex and vibrant network of conscious energies, each radiating unique attributes and qualities. Imagine a vast and multifaceted ocean, where each wave, each current, each sea creature represents a distinct divinity, contributing to the richness and totality of the ecosystem. This is the Celtic pantheon: a myriad of gods and goddesses, beings of power and mystery, whose stories intertwine in a cosmic fabric of epic proportions. Exploring this pantheon is embarking on a journey through a labyrinth of myths and archetypes, where each encounter reveals new perspectives on the nature of the divine and the human condition.

As we approach these divinities, we begin to perceive that they are not mere figures of ancient legends, but rather living forces that permeate reality. They are the primordial energies that shape the cosmos, the sources of power that sustain life and consciousness. These divinities are not organized in a linear and rigid hierarchy, like human power structures, but rather in an intricate web of relationships and interdependencies. Each god and goddess has their own domain and specific attributes, but all are interconnected, contributing to the harmony and dynamic balance of the whole. Understanding this pantheon is not just cataloging names and stories, but rather tuning in to the archetypal energies they represent, and recognizing their subtle, yet profound, influence on our own journey.

One of the striking characteristics of the Celtic pantheon is its fluidity and adaptability. Over time and in different Celtic regions, the names and attributes of the divinities could vary, reflecting cultural nuances and local particularities. However, behind this diversity of names, we can identify archetypes and divine functions that are repeated and manifested in different ways. This flexibility invites us not to see the Celtic pantheon as a static set of fixed entities, but rather as a dynamic and living system, capable of adapting and transforming over time and in different contexts.

Generally, the Celtic pantheon is categorized into large groups of divinities, although the boundaries between these categories are not always clear. One of the most well-known and revered groups is the Tuatha Dé Danann, which can be translated as "People of the Goddess Danu". These are the main gods and goddesses of Irish mythology, considered the divine ancestors of the Irish and associated with magic, wisdom, beauty, art and war. The Tuatha Dé Danann are often described as luminous and powerful beings, who arrived in Ireland from distant lands and brought with them superior knowledge and skills. They represent order, civilization and the forces of light, in contrast to other groups of divinities more associated with chaos and primordial forces.

Among the Tuatha Dé Danann, figures such as Dagda, the "Good God", father of all gods, associated with abundance, wisdom and magic, stand out. Dagda is often represented as a strong and generous being, carrying a magical cauldron that never runs out, a powerful staff and an enchanted harp. He is the protector of the clan, the provider of sustenance and the master of ancestral knowledge. Another central figure is Morrigan, the warrior goddess, associated with battle, destiny and sovereignty. Morrigan is complex and multifaceted, manifesting herself in different forms, such as the crow, the warrior and the wise old woman. She is feared and revered for her strength, her cunning and her ability to influence the course of battles and destiny.

Lugh, the "Bright God", is another prominent member of the Tuatha Dé Danann, associated with sunlight, arts, skills and knowledge. Lugh is considered a master in all arts and crafts, from poetry and music to metallurgy and magic. He is a solar hero, a brilliant warrior and a symbol of excellence and mastery. Brigid, the triple goddess, is revered as the goddess of fire, healing, poetry and childbirth. Brigid manifests in three forms: the maiden, the mother and the crone, representing the different aspects of life and female wisdom. She is the protector of homes, healers, poets and artisans, and is associated with the sacred flame of inspiration and healing.

In addition to the Tuatha Dé Danann, another important group in the Celtic pantheon are the Fomorians. These are often described as older and more primordial divinities, associated with chaos, darkness and the forces of untamed nature. The Fomorians represent the challenges, obstacles and destructive forces that are part of life, but which are also necessary for balance and transformation. In many myths, the Tuatha Dé Danann and the Fomorians face each other in epic battles, representing the struggle between order and chaos, light and darkness, civilization and wild nature.

Cernunnos, the horned god, is another widely revered Celtic divinity, associated with wild nature, animals, fertility, abundance and the cycle of life and death. Cernunnos is often represented as a man with deer antlers, sitting amidst nature, surrounded by animals. He personifies the vital force of nature, the connection with the animal world and the primordial energy of life. Danu, the primordial mother goddess, is considered the ancestor of the Tuatha Dé Danann and the source of life, fertility and nourishment. Danu is a maternal and nurturing figure, associated with fertile land, primordial waters and the abundance of nature.

    The Celtic Gods reveal themselves to be much more than mythological figures from a distant past; they are vibrant archetypes that echo through time, resonating in the depths of the collective unconscious and manifesting in the cultural tapestries that shape our understanding of the world. The diversity and fluidity of the Celtic pantheon, the absence of a rigid hierarchy, and its intrinsic connection with nature, offer a unique perspective on the divine. Each divinity, whether of the luminous Tuatha Dé Danann or the primordial Fomorians, personifies primordial forces and archetypal qualities that intertwine in a cosmic dance of creation and destruction, order and chaos, light and darkness. Understanding Cernunnos is connecting with the vital force of untamed nature, while contemplating Morrigan is confronting the complexity of war, destiny and sovereignty. Lugh radiates the brilliance of intellect and mastery, Dagda personifies abundance and ancestral wisdom, and Brigid ignites the flame of inspiration and healing. By recognizing the interconnection of these divinities, we realize that the Celtic pantheon is not a static collection of isolated characters, but rather a dynamic and interdependent system that reflects the very complexity of existence. This intricate web of divine relationships mirrors our own human journey, with its challenges, ambiguities and potentialities, offering an archetypal mirror to reflect on our own nature and our place in the cosmos.

The relevance of the Celtic Gods transcends the realm of ancient mythology, reaching the spheres of contemporary spirituality and depth psychology. Studying these divinities is not just revisiting ancestral legends, but rather diving into primordial sources of archetypal wisdom that continue to influence our perception of the world and ourselves. The archetypes personified by the Celtic Gods – the solar hero, the warrior goddess, the god of wild nature, the triple goddess – are universal patterns that manifest in diverse cultures and eras, reflecting fundamental aspects of the human experience. By connecting with these archetypal energies, we can gain profound insights into our own inner challenges, our latent talents and our potential for growth. Furthermore, the strong connection of the Celtic pantheon with nature offers a valuable counterpoint to the modern worldview, often disconnected from the natural rhythm and the intrinsic wisdom of the natural world. In times of growing environmental concern and the search for a more grounded spirituality, the Celtic pantheon offers a model of reverence for nature, respect for the cycles of life and death, and recognition of the interconnectedness of all things.

In summary, the study of the Celtic Gods is an invitation to a journey of discovery that takes us beyond the pages of history and leads us to the beating heart of the human experience. These gods and goddesses, with their rich stories and multifaceted personalities, are not mere figures of a remote past, but rather portals to a deeper understanding of ourselves and the world around us. By unraveling the mysteries of the Celtic pantheon, we tune in to the archetypal energies that shaped the worldview of a people and that continue to influence the very fabric of existence. This ancestral legacy offers us a compass to navigate the challenges of the present, a source of inspiration to nurture our spiritual journey, and a mirror to reflect on our own divine nature, intrinsically linked to the cosmic web of life. The voice of the Celtic Gods, whispering through the centuries, invites us to awaken to the magic that permeates the world, to honor the wisdom of nature, and to recognize the divinity that resides in each of us.

Chapter 5
Non-Physical Realities

We emerge from a threshold, driven by the curiosity inherent to our species, questioning the nature of what surrounds us and what constitutes us. In the fabric of existence, we perceive patterns and narratives that echo through time, like whispers of ancestral wisdom. We consider the accounts of those who came before us, the stories that shaped cultures and inspired generations, seeking to discern the essence behind the symbols and metaphors. We immerse ourselves in vibrant belief systems, exploring the richness of pantheons and the divine figures that inhabit them. We contemplate the attributes and legends of these beings of power, seeking to understand their functions and their significance within a vast cosmic order.

As we delve deeper into the tapestry of these spiritual traditions, we inevitably confront inquiries about the dwelling place of these venerated entities. Where are the realms of these gods and goddesses located? On what plane of existence do the energies they personify manifest? The answer, which resonates through diverse currents of mystical and philosophical thought, points to the existence of domains that transcend our immediate perception. These realities, often referred to as "non-physical," suggest a complex and intricate coexistence with our tangible world, operating at frequencies and dimensions that escape the detection of our ordinary senses and conventional scientific instruments.

Thus, we are led to consider the possibility that the reality we apprehend daily is only a portion of a much broader spectrum. Perhaps the universe we know is merely the tip of a cosmic iceberg, immersed in oceans of energies and consciousness that we have not yet fully mapped. The search for understanding these hidden domains becomes, then, an essential journey to expand our cognitive and spiritual horizons. By questioning "where do these divinities reside?", we begin an exploration that will inevitably lead us to unravel the multidimensional nature of reality itself, a concept that challenges the boundaries of our perception and invites us to contemplate the infinite potential of existence.

Our perception of reality is, by nature, limited. Our senses, although sophisticated, capture only a small fraction of the spectrum of energies and frequencies that permeate the universe. Modern science, with its empirical methods and focus on the measurable, concentrates predominantly on the physical world, on the material universe that can be observed, quantified, and tested in the laboratory. This approach, while valuable for understanding the physical world, can lead us to an incomplete view of reality, neglecting the existence of other dimensions and forms of consciousness that do not fit within the parameters of known physics.

Within Celtic spirituality, and in various other shamanic and mystical traditions around the world, reality is understood as multidimensional. It is believed that the physical world, which we perceive with our five senses, is only one layer of existence, a dense and tangible manifestation of subtler energies and forces that operate in other dimensions. These non-physical dimensions are not necessarily distant "places" or spatially separated from our world, but rather realities that interpenetrate ours, vibrating at different frequencies, on planes of existence that escape our linear and three-dimensional perception.

In the Celtic tradition, these non-physical dimensions are often referred to as the "Otherworld" or, in ancient Irish, "Tír na nÓg," the "Land of Youth" or "Avalon" in other narratives. These names evoke a realm of mystery, magic, and beauty, a place where the laws of physics as we know them do not apply, where time and space behave differently, and where consciousness assumes forms and manifestations that transcend biology and matter. The Otherworld is not a distant paradise or a mere abstract concept, but a living and pulsating reality, accessible through altered states of consciousness, rituals, meditative practices, and a deep connection with nature.

The non-physical dimensions are described as inhabited by different forms of consciousness. In addition to the gods and goddesses of the Celtic pantheon, it is believed that these planes of existence are populated by nature spirits, venerated ancestors, fairies, elementals, and other spiritual entities, each with their own nature, purpose, and level of evolution. These forms of consciousness are not necessarily limited to physical bodies like ours, but can exist as pure energy, light, sound, thought, or other manifestations that surpass our linear understanding. It is important to emphasize that these dimensions are no less "real" than our physical world, but different in nature and vibrational frequency. Just as sound and light are different manifestations of the same electromagnetic energy, the physical world and the non-physical dimensions are different expressions of the same fundamental reality.

Communication and interaction with the non-physical dimensions are central elements of Celtic spirituality. Through specific rituals, chants, dances, meditations, shamanic journeys, and other practices, the Celtic disciple seeks to establish bridges between the physical world and the Otherworld, seeking guidance, healing, power, and knowledge from the gods and spirits that inhabit these subtle realities. It is believed that contact with the non-physical dimensions can bring profound benefits to the practitioner's life, expanding their consciousness, awakening intuition, strengthening the connection with nature and the sacred, and providing a deeper understanding of reality and their own purpose in the journey of life.

For the disciple of the Celtic gods, the exploration of non-physical dimensions is not merely an intellectual curiosity, but an essential part of the spiritual path. It is in these dimensions that the gods manifest themselves more directly and powerfully, it is there that we find the realms of magic and transformation, and it is through interaction with these subtle realities that we can accelerate our spiritual growth and fulfill our destiny. However, it is crucial to approach the exploration of non-physical dimensions with respect, reverence, and responsibility. Just as venturing into an unknown forest requires caution and preparation, the journey to the Otherworld demands ethics, sincere intention, and the guidance of experienced guides. The Celtic disciple must seek knowledge, learn the proper practices, cultivate purity of intention, and always act with respect and responsibility when interacting with the energies and entities that inhabit the dimensions beyond ordinary perception.

Contact with the non-physical dimensions, however, is not limited to a set of techniques or rituals; it is, above all, a journey of inner transformation. When venturing into these domains of expanded reality, the individual confronts their own limitations, beliefs, and perceptions. This process of confrontation and subsequent overcoming is intrinsic to spiritual growth. The search for non-physical dimensions reflects, in a way, the journey of the mythical hero, who, upon descending into the underworld or ascending to the heavens, returns transformed, bearing new knowledge and powers. Just as the hero returns to their community with gifts and wisdom, the disciple who explores non-physical realities can bring back valuable insights for their daily life and for the community to which they belong. This journey, however, is not without challenges. The non-physical dimensions, being domains of pure energy and consciousness, can present themselves in unexpected and sometimes challenging ways. It is crucial, therefore, to approach this exploration with discernment, wisdom, and, above all, respect. The search for these realities must be motivated by a genuine desire for spiritual growth and understanding, and not by mere curiosity or the pursuit of personal power. Ethics and pure intention are essential compasses on this inner and outer journey.

The exploration of non-physical realities in the context of Celtic spirituality, and in similar traditions, represents, therefore, an invitation to the expansion of our consciousness and the redefinition of our perception of reality. By recognizing the existence of dimensions that transcend the physical world, we open ourselves to a universe of infinite possibilities. We cease to be confined to the limited vision of the five senses and tangible matter, and begin to glimpse the vast tapestry of existence, where the physical and the non-physical coexist and constantly interpenetrate. This change of perspective has the power to transform our daily lives in profound ways. By understanding that we are multidimensional beings, connected to a web of consciousness and energies that extends beyond what we can see or touch, we find a sense of belonging and purpose much greater. The feeling of isolation and separation, so common in modern human experience, begins to dissipate, giving way to a perception of interconnectedness and unity with all that exists. This expansion of consciousness is not a mere intellectual exercise, but a living and transforming experience that is reflected in all areas of our lives, from our interpersonal relationships to our relationship with the planet and with the cosmos.

Ultimately, the journey through the non-physical dimensions is a journey back home, a reunion with our deepest essence and with the primordial source from which we all emerge. By exploring these subtle domains of reality, we are not only discovering "other worlds," but rediscovering the fullness of our own being. Celtic spirituality, with its emphasis on nature, ancestry, and the interconnectedness of all things, offers us a valuable map for this journey. Through its myths, rituals, and practices, we are invited to awaken to the multidimensional reality that surrounds us and resides within us. And in doing so, we open ourselves to the possibility of living a fuller, more meaningful life in harmony with the cosmic flow of existence. The exploration of non-physical realities is, therefore, not the end of the journey, but the beginning of a continuous path of discovery, growth, and expansion of consciousness, a path that will lead us, inevitably, to a deeper understanding of ourselves and the universe we inhabit.

Chapter 6
From the Irrational to the Divine

Emerging from the mists of the beyond-sense, where the veils of perception dissolve, a central question arises, a perennial enigma that echoes through the ages and spiritual traditions. We now abandon the explorations of the invisible domains, the cartographies of the ancestral pantheon, to immerse ourselves in the beating heart of the spiritual experience itself. What is the essence that animates the search, that directs the yearning for transcendence, that shapes the journey of the spirit? Is consciousness, in its myriad manifestations, the master key that unlocks the mysteries of existence? Let us turn our gaze to this inner universe, this intimate cosmos, to unravel the threads that weave the fabric of our perception and our reality.

Unveiling the nature of consciousness is like peering into a deep and unfathomable ocean, where layer upon layer of reality overlap and interpenetrate. From the most primordial states, where perception manifests as a mere instinctive reflex, an automatic response to external stimuli, to the sublime spheres of divine consciousness, where unity is revealed in its fullness, a vast and complex spectrum extends. For the sincere seeker, for the disciple who yearns to tread the paths of ancestral wisdom, understanding these nuances, discerning the different gradations of consciousness, is not merely an intellectual exercise, but an existential imperative. It is in this knowledge that the compass resides that guides the journey, that illuminates the steps in the labyrinth of the spiritual quest.

The spiritual journey, in its purest essence, reveals itself as an odyssey of consciousness, a progressive expansion of being that tears us away from the shackles of illusion and leads us towards the light of clarity. It is a gradual awakening, an inner blossoming that liberates us from the sleep of ignorance and reveals to us the vastness of wisdom. This path, far from being linear and predictable, unfolds in an ascending spiral, where at each turn we approach the primordial connection with the sacred. Thus, let us immerse ourselves in the exploration of the levels of consciousness, not as mere observers, but as intrepid explorers, unraveling the secrets that lie in the depths of our own being, in search of that divine spark that resides in each of us.

We can conceive of consciousness as a continuous spectrum, which extends from the faintest spark of perception to the vastest and most comprehensive understanding. At one extreme of this spectrum, we find what we can call "irrational consciousness", the state of being predominant in the simplest living beings, such as plants, bacteria, and unicellular organisms. At this level, consciousness manifests primarily as instinct, automatic reaction to the environment, and an incessant search for survival and reproduction. There is a form of perception, a rudimentary sensitivity to external stimuli, but there is no self-awareness, reflection, or capacity for deliberate choice. Life at this level is governed by basic biological impulses, operating in a mode of automatic reaction and response to the world.

Advancing in the spectrum of consciousness, we find the level of "rational consciousness", the state of being that characterizes human beings and other animals with complex nervous systems. At this level, the capacity to think, reason, plan, learn from experience, and develop a sense of individuality and personal identity arises. Rational consciousness allows for the creation of language, culture, society, and technology. It grants us the ability to analyze the world around us, to make conscious choices, to reflect on the past and project the future. Rational consciousness represents a significant evolutionary leap, conferring upon us a remarkable power to shape our environment and our own existence.

However, rational consciousness, by itself, does not represent the apex of spiritual evolution. Although it grants us intellect, logic, and analytical capacity, it can also imprison us in a limited mental world, focused on the ego, separation, and duality. The rational mind, when not balanced by other dimensions of consciousness, can become an instrument of illusion, generating patterns of negative thinking, fears, anxieties, and a sense of disconnection from the whole. The exclusive pursuit of rational knowledge, disconnected from the wisdom of the heart and intuition, can lead us away from the true essence of human experience, leading to a state of alienation and spiritual emptiness.

Beyond rational consciousness, we glimpse the horizon of "spiritual consciousness", a state of being that transcends the limitations of the linear mind and connects with a deeper and more comprehensive reality. Spiritual consciousness is characterized by intuition, innate wisdom, compassion, unconditional love, the sense of unity with the whole, and the perception of the divine presence in all things. At this level of consciousness, the separation between self and other dissolves, duality fades away, and we experience the profound interconnectedness of all existence. Spiritual consciousness allows us to access a knowledge that goes beyond logic and reason, a wisdom that emanates directly from the primordial source of life.

It is important to understand the analogy of the distance that separates an irrational being from a rational being, and the similar distance that exists between a rational being and a spiritually evolved being. Just as an irrational being, guided only by instincts, is incapable of understanding the complexity of rational thought, a human being trapped only in rational consciousness may have difficulty conceiving the vastness and depth of spiritual consciousness. From the perspective of irrational consciousness, the world of human reason may seem abstract, confusing, and incomprehensible. In the same way, from the perspective of purely rational consciousness, the world of spirituality may seem vague, subjective, and devoid of meaning. However, the reality is that each level of consciousness represents a step on an evolutionary ladder, a step towards an increasingly broad and deep understanding of existence.

The journey of the Celtic disciple, therefore, is a journey of ascension on the ladder of consciousness. It is a path that invites us to transcend the limitations of purely rational consciousness and awaken to the potential of spiritual consciousness that resides within us. It is not a matter of denying or rejecting reason, but rather of integrating it into a broader and more comprehensive way of being, which includes intuition, emotion, creativity, and connection with the sacred. The goal is not to abandon the mind, but to transform it into an instrument at the service of a greater purpose, aligned with the values of the soul and with the search for truth and wisdom.

The "awakening of consciousness", a term frequently used in various spiritual traditions, refers precisely to this transition, to this movement from limited rational consciousness to expansive spiritual consciousness. It is a process of recognizing our true spiritual nature, of liberation from the illusory patterns of thought that keep us trapped in a state of suffering and disconnection, and of opening ourselves to the direct experience of divine reality. This awakening is not a single and instantaneous event, but a continuous journey, a process of refinement and expansion of consciousness that extends throughout life.

The search for completeness, therefore, does not reside in stopping at the initial levels of consciousness, whether in irrational impulsivity or purely rational logic. Both, although distinct and necessary stages in the journey of the soul's evolution, represent only transitory moments on the path towards the full expansion of being. Irrational consciousness, useful for basic survival and instinctive interaction with the world, lacks the reflective depth and capacity for conscious choice that mark the human experience in its complexity. Rational consciousness, with its analytical power and capacity to construct elaborate systems of thought, can, paradoxically, become a prison if we neglect the more subtle dimensions of our existence. By identifying ourselves exclusively with the rational mind, we run the risk of isolating ourselves from intuitive richness, the innate wisdom of the heart, and the deep connection with the interconnected fabric of life. True mastery, the pinnacle of the Celtic disciple's journey, lies in the ability to integrate these different facets of consciousness, allowing reason to serve as a valuable instrument, but without it becoming the dominant force that obscures the perception of the spiritual vastness that awaits us.

The awakening of consciousness, in this context, arises as a call to transcendence, an invitation to cross the limiting boundaries of the linear mind and explore the unexplored territories of spiritual consciousness. It is not a matter of abandoning reason, but of placing it at the service of a greater purpose, of integrating it into a broader and more compassionate worldview. The awakened individual understands that reality is multifaceted, that truth is not restricted to the limits of logical thought, and that genuine wisdom emanates from a source that transcends the intellect. This awakening is a continuous process, a journey of refinement and expansion of perception that unfolds throughout life. At each step on this journey, the veil of illusion becomes thinner, understanding deepens, and the sense of unity with the whole intensifies. The individual realizes that the separation between self and other is a mental construct, a mirage of the rational mind, and that, in essence, we are all interconnected, weaving together the fabric of existence. This perception of interconnectedness generates compassion, unconditional love, and a deep sense of responsibility towards the world and towards all the beings that inhabit it.

The journey of the Celtic disciple, this incessant search for the expansion of consciousness, is an odyssey towards our own divine essence. It is a return to the primordial source of life, a reconnection with the spark of light that resides in each of us. This path is not without challenges and obstacles. The rational mind, with its ingrained patterns of thought and its tendency to resist the unknown, can present itself as a formidable opponent. However, by persisting in the search, by cultivating intuition, meditation, and the practice of conscious presence, we gradually transcend the limitations of the mind and open ourselves to the vastness of spiritual consciousness. In this state of expanded being, we experience a deep peace, an unconditional joy, and a sense of purpose and meaning that permeates every aspect of our existence. The journey of consciousness, therefore, is not just an individual search, but a contribution to the collective evolution of humanity, a step towards a brighter and more harmonious future for all.

Chapter 7
The Call to the Disciple

In the exploration of the soul, in the mapping of the spirit and in the investigation of consciousness, understanding expands, revealing the complexities of the human experience. We arrive at a point of transformation that directs us to a new dimension of exploration. Leaving behind the initial premises, we enter a deeper domain, contemplating not only the journey, but the direction that manifests ahead.

A unique horizon unfolds: the path of discipleship. Not as an imposition, but as an inner invitation, a resonance that emanates from the being. It is the recognition of an individual path, which beckons with the promise of transformation and communion with the transcendent. It is not an audible call, but an awakening of consciousness, which reconfigures the perception of reality and the mystery of existence. It manifests as a subtle attraction, a magnetism of the soul towards the deep and meaningful.

The nature of this convocation reveals itself in diverse ways, in multiple channels of experience, without a single pattern. For some, it arises as a persistent feeling of incompleteness, an indefinable yearning for a meaning that transcends materiality. For others, it erupts through an unexpected encounter, a sudden connection with the ancestral legacy, whether through words, melodies, places or experiences that trigger an internal recognition, illuminating the path of the search.

This call can manifest in various forms, often subtle and indirect. For some, it manifests as a persistent feeling of emptiness and dissatisfaction with modern life, a yearning for something deeper and more meaningful that transcends routine. For others, it may arise through a chance encounter with Celtic culture, whether through reading, traditional music, visiting historical or natural sites, or any experience that awakens an inner resonance. Still others, the call may manifest as a vivid dream, a strong intuition, a striking synchronicity or an inexplicable feeling of familiarity and belonging to the Celtic world.

Regardless of the form, the call to the disciple is always a personal and intimate experience. It arises from within, from the heart of the soul, like a gentle voice that invites one to a journey of self-discovery and spiritual connection. It is not an imposition, but an appeal that resonates with the deep essence, awakening a yearning for something more authentic than everyday life offers. Answering this call is a free choice, a decision to follow a direction that reveals itself to be true for the soul.

It is important to distinguish this inner call from mere passing curiosities. The true call to the disciple is persistent, profound and transformative. It is not limited to an intellectual interest or aesthetic attraction, but to a yearning that drives one to seek deep knowledge, practice rituals with sincere intention, incorporate values and build a genuine relationship with the divinities. The true disciple responds to the call with an open heart, a curious mind and the willingness to dedicate oneself to a path of spiritual growth and devotional service.

Sincere intention is fundamental in responding to the call. Curiosity is not enough, it is necessary to cultivate a clear and authentic intention, a genuine desire to learn, practice and connect with the divinities. Intention is the compass that guides the spiritual journey, the engine of practice and the strength of devotion. A sincere intention attracts the attention and blessing of the divinities, facilitating progress. A confused or superficial intention can lead one astray from the true path.

Free will is crucial on the spiritual journey. The decision to answer the call is always individual. The divinities offer presence, wisdom and help, but they respect the freedom of choice and the individual rhythm of learning and growth. The path of spirituality is of free and spontaneous will, renewed at each step. To respect free will is to recognize the validity of many spiritual paths and the right of each one to choose what best resonates with the soul. The beauty of spirituality resides in the diversity of paths and in the freedom to find one's own connection with the divine.

The first step on the disciple's journey is to open oneself to the possibility. To allow oneself to explore the culture, mythology, philosophy and spiritual practices with an open mind and receptive heart. Reading, researching, participating in groups, conversing with experienced practitioners, visiting places of worship and experimenting with rituals and meditations are ways to begin this exploration. In the beginning, the most important thing is to cultivate curiosity, humility and a willingness to learn. It is not necessary to have all the answers immediately, nor to feel pressured to adopt specific beliefs or practices. Discovery is gradual and continuous, and the disciple's journey begins with a simple step: opening the heart and mind to the possibility that this path may resonate with the soul.

This introduction to the path of the disciple is an invitation to reflect on the inner call, to discern the authenticity of this call and to take the first step towards a journey of self-discovery and spiritual connection. Knowledge about the divinities, rituals, devotional practices and ancestral philosophy offers a practical and inspiring guide for those who feel the call to become disciples in the modern world. May this knowledge be a faithful companion on this journey, illuminating the path with ancestral wisdom and the strength of tradition.

In short, the nature of the call to discipleship unfolds as an intimate and personal invitation that resonates in the depths of the soul. Far from imposition or fashion, this appeal manifests in myriad ways, from the feeling of incompleteness to fortuitous encounters that ignite ancestral recognition. It is crucial to discern the authenticity of this call, separating it from ephemeral curiosities and embracing sincere intention as a compass. Free will emerges as a fundamental pillar, reiterating that the response is a sovereign choice, respected by the divinities, who offer presence and wisdom, without imposing devotion. The first step resides in opening oneself to the possibility, in allowing oneself to explore the richness of culture, mythology and practices with genuine curiosity and humility, ready to tread a path of self-discovery and spiritual connection that begins with an act of surrender and receptivity.

The journey of discipleship is configured as a continuous and gradual search, where self-knowledge and spiritual connection are intertwined. The disciple, upon answering the call, embarks on a path of internal and external exploration, armed with an open heart, an inquisitive mind and a willingness to learn. This path is not linear, but spiral, permeated by discoveries, challenges and introspection. The beauty of spirituality lies in the ability to embrace the diversity of individual paths, respecting the rhythm of each seeker and the myriad forms in which the sacred manifests itself. Thus, discipleship is not imposed as a single model, but flourishes in the freedom to find one's own devotional expression, nurturing a genuine relationship with the divinities and ancestral wisdom.

This starting point serves as an entry portal for those who feel the call, offering an initial compass for the first steps on the disciple's journey. By deepening ancestral knowledge, exploring the pantheon of divinities, rituals and devotional practices, and diving into the philosophy that sustains this tradition, this knowledge serves as a beacon to illuminate the path of those who feel called to tread the path of discipleship, guided by ancestral wisdom and strengthened by the profound connection with spirituality, finding in this journey a deeper meaning for existence and a blossoming of the soul towards the light of the transcendent.

Chapter 8
Dagda
The Good God, the Father of All

Here begins a journey through the veils that separate the tangible world from the ethereal dimensions, an invitation to peer into the primordial forces that shape existence. After delving into the depths of the ancestral call and the principles that sustain the spirituality of a people, we are now compelled to direct our gaze towards the luminous entities that inhabit the heart of this tradition. These divine figures, shrouded in mystery and reverence, personify cosmic archetypes, manifestations of power and wisdom that echo through time. Approaching these presences is not configured as mere mythological contemplation, but rather as an act of recognizing the intricate web of energies that permeate the universe and influence the individual path on the spiritual journey.

Within this vast and complex panorama, the singular figure of Dagda emerges, a name that resonates with the force of an ancestral thunder and the softness of a paternal breeze. Recognized as "The Good God" and "Father of All," Dagda is not limited to a mere hierarchical title, but rather radiates the very essence of divine benevolence. His presence manifests in the abundance of nature, in the safety of homes, in the ancestral wisdom that guides hesitant steps. He is the primordial source of provision, the tireless protector against adversities, the beacon of knowledge that illuminates the journey in the search for understanding. Entering the universe of Dagda is, therefore, connecting with an inexhaustible source of primordial virtues, a central archetype in the spiritual worldview that we are now unraveling.

Understanding the depth of Dagda transcends the mere analysis of attributes and symbols; it implies recognizing the reverberation of his archetypal energy in the core of human experience. For the contemporary seeker, Dagda presents himself as a guide and protector, a source of inspiration to cultivate active goodness, inner strength and innate wisdom. As we approach the essence of Dagda, we open a portal to access an ancestral legacy of power and knowledge, an invitation to integrate into our personal journey the principles that emanate from this divine archetype, thus treading the path of spiritual evolution with confidence and purpose.

Dagda, in his essence, represents goodness in its most primordial and comprehensive form. His epithet "The Good God" does not refer to a passive or naive goodness, but rather to an active and generous force that seeks the well-being and prosperity of all creation. He is the provider, the protector, the wise guide, the one who offers sustenance, security and knowledge to his sons and daughters. His goodness manifests in the abundance of nature, in the fertility of the land, in the richness of harvests and in the prosperity of herds. He is the personification of divine generosity, the source of gift and blessing that nurtures and sustains life in all its forms.

As "Father of All," Dagda occupies a prominent position in the Celtic divine hierarchy, being considered the leader and patriarch of the Tuatha Dé Danann. His paternity, however, transcends the idea of an authoritarian and distant figure. Dagda is a present, accessible and compassionate father, who cares about the well-being of his sons and daughters, both divine and human. He is the protector of the tribe, the wise leader who guides and orients, the loving father who offers support and comfort in times of difficulty. His paternity manifests in the protection, guidance, care and unconditional love that he bestows upon all who seek his aid.

The attributes and symbols associated with Dagda reflect his multifaceted and powerful nature. One of his most emblematic symbols is the cauldron of abundance, a magical object that is never exhausted, capable of providing food and drink for all, in unlimited quantity. This cauldron represents the inexhaustible generosity of Dagda, his ability to provide sustenance and abundance for all who need it. It symbolizes the abundance of nature, the promise that basic needs will always be met, and the belief in the divine provision that sustains life.

Another striking attribute of Dagda is his powerful club, a formidable weapon that he wields with mastery. This club represents his strength, his power of protection and his ability to ward off the forces of chaos and destruction. It is not a weapon of aggression or excessive violence, but rather an instrument of defense and justice, used to protect his loved ones and maintain order and balance in the cosmos. Dagda's club symbolizes the protective force of the father, the security he offers against external threats, and the firmness necessary to maintain harmony and justice.

Dagda's magic harp is another important symbol, representing his wisdom, his poetry and his mastery over the arts. This enchanted harp was capable of playing melodies that influenced people's emotions and state of mind, bringing joy, sadness, sleep or even healing. Dagda's harp symbolizes his ability to influence the world through music, poetry and beauty, revealing the importance of arts and culture in Celtic spirituality. It also represents ancestral wisdom, the deep knowledge that resides in Dagda's heart, capable of harmonizing and healing through sound and melody.

Dagda's domains are vast and comprehensive, reflecting his central position in the Celtic pantheon. He is considered the god of wisdom, holder of a deep and ancestral knowledge that encompasses all areas of life and the universe. He is also the god of magic, master of the occult arts and capable of performing extraordinary feats through magical power. Dagda is the god of abundance, provider of plenty, prosperity and sustenance for all. He is the god of protection, guardian of the tribe and defender against the forces of evil. And, above all, Dagda is the god of ancestral knowledge, the guardian of traditions, myths and wisdom passed down from generation to generation.

The myths and stories associated with Dagda reveal his wisdom, his power and his multifaceted nature. In many narratives, he appears as a shrewd and strategic leader, capable of solving complex problems and overcoming seemingly insurmountable challenges. His wisdom is often demonstrated in his negotiations with other divinities, in his war strategies and in his wise and just decisions. His strength and power are evident in his battles against the forces of chaos and destruction, where he always emerges victorious, protecting his people and restoring order and balance. And his goodness and generosity are revealed in his gifts and blessings, in his abundant provision and in his paternal care for all beings.

Connecting with Dagda in rituals and devotional practices is to seek his guidance, his protection and his blessings of abundance and wisdom. We can invoke Dagda in times when we need strength, courage, protection or wise guidance. We can ask for his help to overcome challenges, solve problems, find creative solutions and make important decisions. We can honor him with offerings of food and drink, such as milk, honey, bread and fruit, symbolizing his generosity and our gratitude for his provision. We can meditate on his symbols, such as the cauldron, the club and the harp, seeking his energy and inspiration. And we can simply spend time in nature, in places of abundance and beauty, feeling his presence in the richness of the land, in the strength of the trees and in the ancestral wisdom of the landscape.

In this way, the figure of Dagda is not confined to the ancestral Celtic pantheon, but radiates its influence beyond time, reaching the contemporary seeker who longs to anchor his spiritual journey in solid and archetypal principles. By internalizing the essence of Dagda, the individual is invited to cultivate active goodness in his actions, to manifest inner strength in the face of challenges, and to seek the innate wisdom that resides in his own being. Dagda's symbols, such as the cauldron of abundance, the powerful club and the magic harp, transcend mere mythological representation, becoming keys of understanding for the personal journey. The cauldron evokes the importance of generosity and sharing, remembering that true wealth lies in the ability to provide and nurture others. The club, in turn, symbolizes the need to protect one's own limits and to defend what is right, using force with discernment and responsibility. The magic harp, on the other hand, echoes the power of harmony, beauty and creative expression as pathways to healing and spiritual elevation, encouraging the search for beauty and art as food for the soul.

Thus, when contemplating the vastness of Dagda's domains and the richness of his attributes, we are invited to perceive his presence as a guiding beacon in the intricate journey of existence. Dagda, as an archetype of primordial goodness and universal paternity, offers an inspiring model for the construction of a spirituality anchored in generosity, protection and ancestral wisdom. The connection with the energy of Dagda can be cultivated through the appreciation of nature in its beauty and abundance, the practice of active goodness in everyday life, and the search for knowledge and harmony in all dimensions of life. By opening ourselves to the archetypal influence of Dagda, we establish a link with the primordial force that sustains creation, nurturing the spiritual journey with confidence, purpose and the certainty that, under the protection of the "Good God" and "Father of All," the path of evolution is revealed with clarity and abundance. In this sense, Dagda remains a living and vibrant presence, an ancestral guide whose wisdom echoes through time, inviting each seeker to unravel the unlimited potential of goodness, strength and knowledge that resides within their own interior.

Dagda's legacy transcends myths and legends, manifesting itself as a timeless legacy of universal principles. By embracing the teachings implicit in the figure of Dagda, the individual is invited to tread a path of integrity, generosity and wisdom, nurturing his own spiritual journey with the primordial force that emanates from this divine archetype. Dagda, the "Good God" and "Father of All," remains a perennial symbol of active goodness, paternal protection and ancestral knowledge, guiding those who seek connection with the primordial forces that shape existence and inspiring the manifestation of human potential in its fullness. His story and his attributes resonate through time, inviting each seeker to recognize the importance of goodness, inner strength and wisdom in the journey of life, and to integrate these principles into his own spiritual path, treading the path of evolution with confidence and inspiration, under the protective and benevolent aegis of Dagda.

Chapter 9
Morrigan
The Goddess of War, Destiny and Sovereignty

In a continuous flow of ancestral energy, after immersing ourselves in the vital and generous currents radiated by the figure of Dagda, we are now led to contemplate another vertex of power and enigma within the Celtic tapestry: Morrigan. Emerging from the mists of time, Morrigan presents herself not as an entity of defined contours, but as a primordial force, an energetic vortex that pulses through the visible and invisible realms. Her essence echoes in the battlefields and the secret corners of the soul, manifesting as a dynamic principle that governs the intricate dance between destiny, sovereignty, and the transforming currents of existence. Entering the domain of Morrigan is to begin a journey through a labyrinth of symbols and archetypes, an invitation to unravel the mysteries that reside in the pulsating heart of reality itself.

As we scrutinize the multifaceted nature of Morrigan, we perceive that she transcends linear definitions, defying simplistic categorizations. She is not limited to personifying war in its rawest manifestation, but embodies the very dynamics of transformation that emerges from confrontations, the incessant struggle for the conquest of inner autonomy and the resistance against the forces that seek to unbalance the cosmic order. Morrigan reveals herself as the strategic mind behind military maneuvers, the astuteness that precedes the attack, the intrepidity that inflames warrior hearts, and the avenging fury that rises in defense of what is essential and right. Her presence on the stages of battle is not restricted to mere destruction, but acts as a catalyzing agent of profound changes, preparing the ground for the gestation of a new configuration, for the eternal cycle of reconstruction and revitalization. Morrigan's war is, ultimately, the war of life itself, the perpetual struggle between the polarities that drive evolution and the constant metamorphosis of being.

However, Morrigan's influence extends far beyond the domains of war. She is intrinsically intertwined with the fabric of destiny, manipulating the threads of wyrd, the invisible web that connects all beings and events in a network of cosmic interdependence. Morrigan holds the gift of prophecy, the penetrating vision that crosses the barriers of time, unraveling the potential paths and the inevitable consequences of each choice. Her understanding of destiny does not manifest as an inflexible determinism, but as the acute perception of the profound connection between all the elements of the universe, of the reverberation of our actions in the future and the importance of being aware of the subtle energies that shape our trajectory. Morrigan calls us to assume responsibility for our own wyrd, to act with clear intention and refined discernment, and to recognize the inherent power in our hands to influence the course of our individual and collective journey.

Morrigan is not a goddess of war in the simplistic sense of gratuitous violence or unbridled carnage. Her war is the war of transformation, the battle for inner sovereignty, the struggle against the forces that threaten order and balance. She is the goddess of military strategy, of astute tactics, of indomitable courage, and of the warrior fury that arises in defense of what is just and necessary. Her presence on the battlefields is not only destructive, but also a catalyst for change, clearing the ground for the emergence of a new order, for rebirth and renewal. Morrigan's war is the war of life, the constant struggle between opposing forces that drive evolution and transformation.

Morrigan is also deeply connected to destiny, weaving the threads of wyrd, the web of fate that connects all beings and events. She is the goddess of prophecy, of the clear vision that penetrates the veils of time, revealing the possible paths and the consequences of choices. Her understanding of destiny is not fatalistic or deterministic, but rather a perception of the interconnection of everything, of the influence of our actions on the future and of the importance of being aware of the forces that shape our path. Morrigan invites us to take responsibility for our destiny, to act with intention and discernment, and to recognize the power that resides in our hands to influence the course of our own journey.

Sovereignty is another fundamental domain of Morrigan. She is the personification of female sovereignty, of the power to govern oneself, to claim one's inner authority and to exert influence in the world with integrity and strength. Her sovereignty is not based on domination or control, but rather on self-confidence, autonomy, and the ability to lead with wisdom and justice. Morrigan inspires us to seek our own inner sovereignty, to free ourselves from the shackles of dependence and submission, and to become lords and ladies of our own destiny, guided by our inner compass and our connection with the sacred.

Morrigan manifests in diverse forms and appearances, reflecting her complex and multifaceted nature. She is often associated with crows and ravens, birds of ill omen in some cultures, but which for the Celts symbolized prophecy, intelligence, and connection with the spiritual world. Morrigan's raven form represents her ability to move between worlds, to observe events from a superior perspective and to foresee the future. The image of the raven flying over the battlefield also evokes her presence in moments of transformation and renewal, announcing both death and rebirth.

Morrigan is also frequently represented as a warrior, dressed in armor and wielding weapons, ready for battle. This warrior form personifies her strength, her courage and her determination to defend what is just and necessary. The image of the warrior Morrigan inspires bravery, self-confidence and the ability to face life's challenges with resilience and determination. It is not an image of gratuitous aggressiveness, but rather of inner strength and readiness to act in defense of values and principles.

Another form of manifestation of Morrigan is that of a wise old woman, an elder holding a deep knowledge and ancestral wisdom. In this form, Morrigan reveals her prophetic face, her ability to see beyond the veil of illusion and to discern the patterns of destiny. The old wise woman Morrigan represents the wisdom of age, the experience accumulated over many lives, and the ability to offer guidance and wise advice in moments of crossroads. This form invites us to seek inner wisdom, to trust our intuition and to learn from the cycles of life and death.

The attributes and symbols of Morrigan are equally rich and evocative. The spear is one of her most important symbols, representing her warrior strength, her strategic precision and her ability to direct energy to a specific purpose. The cauldron of transformation, also associated with Morrigan, symbolizes her ability to catalyze change, to transform death into rebirth and to generate new possibilities from destruction. The raven, as already mentioned, is a central symbol of Morrigan, representing her prophecy, her intelligence and her connection with the spiritual world.

Morrigan's domains encompass war, destiny, sovereignty, magic, prophecy, protection, and the cycle of life and death. She is invoked in moments of conflict, to obtain victory and protection, to seek guidance on the future, to strengthen personal sovereignty and to face the challenges of transformation and change. Morrigan is not an easy goddess to deal with, her energy is intense and challenging, but her presence is always transforming and empowering.

The myths and stories of Morrigan reveal her complexity and her power. She appears in several narratives of the Irish mythological cycle, often playing a crucial role in battles and events that shape the destiny of gods and heroes. Her presence is often associated with moments of crisis and transformation, where she acts as a catalyst for change, challenging the status quo and opening the way for new possibilities. Her wisdom is tested in riddles and challenges, her strength is demonstrated in epic battles, and her sovereignty is claimed with courage and determination.

Connecting with Morrigan in rituals and devotional practices is to seek her strength, her courage, her guidance and her protection in moments of challenge and transformation. We can invoke Morrigan when we face internal or external battles, when we need clarity about our destiny, when we seek to strengthen our personal sovereignty or when we find ourselves in moments of transition and change. We can offer Morrigan offerings that reflect her warrior and sovereign nature, such as raven feathers, symbolic weapons, dragon's blood (red resin) or red wine. We can meditate on her symbols, such as the spear, the cauldron and the raven, seeking her energy and inspiration. And we can honor her through acts of courage, justice and defense of our values and principles.

In a world where dualities intertwine and the search for meaning intensifies, the figure of Morrigan resurfaces not only as a mythological relic, but as a living, vibrant and deeply relevant archetype. As we revisit the multiple aspects of this Celtic Goddess - her warrior facet, her mastery over destiny, the strength of her sovereignty and the ancestral wisdom that emanates from her manifestations - we realize that Morrigan offers us a mirror to understand the complexities of human existence. She confronts us with the inevitability of change, the need for courage in the face of challenges and the importance of taking responsibility for our own path. Far from being just a divinity of the Celtic pantheon, Morrigan personifies primordial forces that continue to shape the fabric of reality, inviting us to a deep dialogue with the transforming energies that drive life in its cycles of destruction and rebirth. Thus, the journey through the Morrigan enigma does not end in the pages of myths, but extends to the core of our own journey, inciting us to unravel the warriors and sovereigns asleep within us.

The essential message of Morrigan, therefore, transcends the battlefields and the veils of prophecy, echoing in every quest for authenticity and personal power. She reminds us that true sovereignty does not reside in dominion over others, but in the conquest of ourselves, in the ability to govern our own energies and intentions. Morrigan's war, in its essence, is a call to inner action, an invitation to confront the shadows that limit us and to fight for the truths we hold essential. By honoring her energy, we are not worshiping gratuitous violence, but rather connecting with the primordial force that drives us to overcome obstacles, to defend our values, and to position ourselves with courage and integrity on the stage of life. In this sense, Morrigan presents herself as a powerful guide for those seeking to strengthen their autonomy, enhance their intuition, and tread a path with purpose and determination, recognizing the constant dance between the forces of creation and destruction as inherent to the journey of the soul.

Ultimately, Morrigan's legacy is one of empowerment and transformation. She calls upon us to embrace the totality of our nature, to recognize the importance of both light and shadow, strength and vulnerability, war and peace. By integrating Morrigan's teachings into our journey, we are invited to develop a deeper vision of destiny, not as something predetermined and inflexible, but as a dynamic flow influenced by our choices and intentions. Morrigan inspires us to be warriors of our own lives, to defend our inner truth with passion and courage, to reclaim our sovereignty with wisdom and justice, and to embrace the perpetual cycle of transformation as the essence of existence. Thus, as we contemplate the intricate tapestry of Morrigan, we find not only a Goddess of War, Destiny, and Sovereignty, but an ancestral mirror that reflects the infinite potential for transformation and power that resides within each of us.

Chapter 10
Lugh
The Brilliant God, Master of Arts

Amidst the ancient annals, where echoes of battles and resonances of power still vibrate, we are now guided to a point of luminous convergence. After the immersion in complex webs of strategy and royalty, the compass of our exploration points to the advent of a manifestation of singular brilliance. No longer the twilight of war, but the dawn of an era of mastery and light. A figure projects itself, adorned with the radiance of the rising sun, radiating not only warmth, but the promise of multifaceted wisdom, a dominion over the arts that transcends the common.

At this threshold of perception, we abandon the shadows to enter a realm where the clarity of knowledge and the strength of creativity come together in a symphony of unlimited potential. Let us prepare, therefore, to contemplate a beacon of excellence, a guide in the intricate paths of human improvement.

The essence that is now revealed pulsates with a vibrant frequency, an energy flow that resonates like the very pulse of the sun. Imagine primordial light condensed, not only in its physical form, but in its ability to illuminate the mind and nurture the soul. From this source emanates a spectrum of qualities that encompass the totality of human expression. It is not limited to a single art or discipline, but manifests itself as a paradigm of comprehensive expertise. A domain that extends from the subtlety of melody to the precision of strategy, from the art of healing to the elocution of the word. This figure presents itself as a living compendium of skills, an archetype of mastery in its most complete and radiant form.

Emerges, then, the name that resonates through the ages, whispered in legends and engraved in archetypes: Lugh. The epithet that precedes him, "Brilliant," is not mere adornment, but the very declaration of his intrinsic nature. He is the light that dispels the shadows of ignorance, the beacon that guides through confusion, the promise of a new dawn of understanding. Not only light, but "Master of Arts," a title that echoes the vastness of his domain. In his essence, Lugh embodies the luminous confluence of knowledge, inventiveness and consummate expertise. To understand Lugh is, therefore, to enter a path of self-improvement, to follow a journey guided by an archetype of excellence. He presents himself as a guide for those who seek to ignite their own flame of creativity, refine dormant skills and project the unique light of their talent into the world.

Lugh is, in his essence, the personification of light. His epithet "Brilliant" evokes solar radiation, the luminosity that dispels darkness and reveals the beauty and clarity of the world. His energy is associated with the sun, the primordial source of life and energy, the star that illuminates, warms and nourishes all creation. Lugh represents the light of reason, knowledge, inspiration and creativity, the force that dispels ignorance, confusion and obscurity. His presence brings clarity, discernment, vitality and the promise of a new dawn, of a future illuminated by knowledge and excellence.

As "Master of Arts," Lugh personifies mastery in all skills and crafts. He is not a specialist in just one art, but a divine polymath, possessing unparalleled knowledge and expertise in all areas of human and divine knowledge. From poetry and music to metallurgy and magic, through military strategy and healing, Lugh masters all the arts with perfection and elegance. He is the patron of artisans, artists, poets, musicians, skilled warriors, healers and all those who seek to improve their abilities and express their talent in the world. His mastery inspires the pursuit of excellence, the development of human potential and the celebration of creativity in all its forms.

The attributes and symbols associated with Lugh reflect his solar and multifaceted nature. The spear is one of his most prominent symbols, representing his precision, his aim and his directed force. Lugh's spear is not only a weapon of combat, but also an instrument of precision and focus, symbolizing his ability to direct energy, to achieve goals with clarity and determination, and to penetrate the depths of knowledge. It represents mental clarity, the ability to concentrate and the capacity to direct talent and energy to achieve mastery.

The raven is another animal associated with Lugh, symbolizing his intelligence, his cunning and his connection with hidden knowledge. The raven, messenger between worlds, represents Lugh's ability to transit between ordinary reality and the realms of inspiration and divine wisdom. It symbolizes perspicacity, sharp intelligence, the ability to observe and learn, and the connection with intuition and knowledge that transcends linear reason.

The sun, naturally, is a central symbol of Lugh, representing his vital energy, his radiant light and his dominion over the day and clarity. The sun symbolizes the energy, vitality, creative force, inspiration and mental clarity that Lugh radiates. It represents the source of light that dispels the darkness of ignorance and confusion, revealing the path of wisdom and mastery. Lugh's solar image evokes the vibrant and positive energy that drives creativity, action and the pursuit of knowledge.

Lugh's domains are vast and reflect his universal mastery. He is the god of the sun and light, radiating vital energy and clarity to the world. He is the god of inspiration and creativity, source of innovative ideas, art and creative expression in all its forms. Lugh is the god of healing, possessing knowledge of herbs, energies and techniques of physical, emotional and spiritual healing. He is the god of journeys, protector of travelers and guide on physical and spiritual journeys. Lugh is the god of communication, master of the word, eloquence, poetry and persuasion. And, above all, Lugh is the god of knowledge, holder of ancestral wisdom, erudition in all areas and the incessant pursuit of learning and understanding.

The myths and stories associated with Lugh reveal his brilliance, his intelligence and his mastery in various areas. One of the most famous stories is that of his entry into Tara, the court of the Tuatha Dé Danann. Lugh was only admitted after demonstrating mastery in various arts, surpassing all others in skill and knowledge. This narrative emphasizes his universal mastery and the importance of talent and expertise in Celtic culture. Other myths narrate his victories in battles, using his strategic intelligence and his warrior skills to overcome powerful enemies. His stories celebrate excellence, the ability to overcome challenges through talent and knowledge, and the importance of the constant pursuit of personal improvement.

Connecting with Lugh in rituals and devotional practices is to seek his inspiration, his guidance and his help in the development of our own abilities and creative talents. We can invoke Lugh when we need inspiration for artistic projects, to overcome creative blocks, to learn new skills or to improve those we already possess. We can ask for his help to develop mental clarity, concentration and the ability to communicate effectively. We can honor him with offerings that reflect his solar and artistic nature, such as golden candles, frankincense, handicrafts, poems or music created in his honor. We can meditate on his symbols, such as the spear, the raven and the sun, seeking his energy and inspiration. And we can dedicate time to the development of our own skills and talents, seeking excellence in everything we do, as a way to honor Lugh's mastery.

Lugh's attributes converge to form an archetype of power and perennial inspiration. His multifaceted nature, which consecrates him as the Brilliant God and Master of all Arts, is revealed not only in the vastness of his domains, but also in the depth of his influence. As we recapitulate the symbols that represent him - the unerring spear, the insightful raven, and the radiant sun - we apprehend the essence of a power that is simultaneously directed, intelligent and illuminating. The spear symbolizes the ability to focus energy and achieve objectives with precision, the raven represents sagacity and connection with hidden knowledge, while the sun personifies the primordial source of life, energy and clarity. These elements, intrinsically linked to Lugh, paint the portrait of a divinity that is not limited to a single aspect of existence, but encompasses the totality of human potential, serving as a beacon for those who aspire to mastery in any field of knowledge or creativity. The figure of Lugh transcends the mere representation of a solar god; he embodies the promise of an awakening to the latent capacities in each individual, a constant invitation to the pursuit of excellence and the celebration of inner light.

The invocation of Lugh is not restricted to mere rituals or formal devotional practices; it represents an invitation to immersion in a continuous process of self-improvement. By connecting with the essence of Lugh, whether through meditation on his symbols, artistic creation in his honor, or the simple dedication to the improvement of our skills, we open ourselves to a flow of inspiration and invaluable guidance. Lugh emerges as a silent mentor, an archetypal guide who encourages us to overcome creative blocks, to develop mental clarity and to communicate our ideas effectively. He personifies the belief in unlimited human potential and in the ability of each individual to ignite their own creative flame and project the unique light of their talent into the world. His mastery in all the arts serves as a constant reminder that specialization should not limit the search for a comprehensive and multifaceted knowledge. On the contrary, Lugh inspires the exploration of diverse areas of knowledge, encouraging the acquisition of an expertise that transcends disciplinary boundaries, and that manifests itself in a holistic and integrated understanding of the world.

In short, the figure of Lugh emerges as an ancestral legacy of invaluable worth to contemporary society. His representation as the Brilliant God, Master of Arts, resonates through time as a timeless archetype of excellence, creativity and knowledge. Lugh is not merely a distant mythological character, but rather an archetypal guide who invites us to tread a path of constant personal and professional refinement. By internalizing his attributes and seeking his inspiration, we are driven to develop our own maximum potential, to celebrate creativity in all its forms, and to radiate our unique light in the world. Lugh's message is clear and inspiring: mastery is not a final destination, but rather a continuous journey of learning, improvement and self-expression, guided by the incessant pursuit of knowledge and by the celebration of the light that resides within each of us.

Chapter 11
Brigid
The Triple Goddess of Fire, Healing, and Poetry

Here unfolds before us the study of an ancestral presence, a force that resonates through time, invoked under multiple names and manifestations. We speak of a generative principle, a primordial energy that reveals itself in the very essence of existence. We are not limited to an isolated mythological figure, but rather to a profound archetype, a matrix of power and wisdom that interweaves with the tapestry of reality itself. This principle, which we will now seek to unveil, is recognized for its multifaceted nature, a reflection of the complexity inherent in the universe we inhabit.

As we examine the layers that make up this entity, we realize that its influence extends to fundamental domains of human and cosmic experience. She presents herself as the very life flame, the heat that nourishes and transforms, the glow that illuminates the darkness. She is the energy that drives renewal, the driving force behind healing and restoration, the creative impetus that manifests in art and expression. In her essence, she represents the convergence of these primordial powers, a triad of interconnected forces that emanate from the same source. Understanding her invites us to explore the depths of our own nature and to recognize the subtle energies that shape our inner and outer world.

In this dive into the core of this archetype, we unveil a guide for those who seek more than the tangible, a beacon for those who yearn for healing in all dimensions, protection against adversity, and the spark of inspiration that ignites the flame of the soul. To approach this force is to walk a path of encounter with one's own vitality, a journey towards connection with the invisible web that unites all things. It is to enter a universe of deep compassion, where the nurturing and creative feminine energy manifests in its fullness, offering a portal to ancestral wisdom and to the recognition of the sacred that resides in every aspect of existence.

Brigid, in her triple essence, manifests in three distinct, yet interconnected, forms, each representing a fundamental aspect of her divine nature and of human experience. These three manifestations are not separate goddesses, but rather facets of the same divinity, expressing the complexity and totality of Brigid's energy. The Maiden, the first face of Brigid, represents the fire of the hearth, the fire of the home, the sacred flame that warms, illuminates, and protects the domestic space. She embodies purity, beginning, potential, and the promise of new beginnings. Maiden Brigid is the guardian of the home, the protector of the family, the goddess of hospitality and warmth, offering security and nourishment in the sacred space of the home.

The Mother, the second face of Brigid, represents the fire of healing, the vital energy that restores health, wholeness, and well-being. She embodies fertility, nourishment, maternal care, and the ability to generate life and healing. Mother Brigid is the goddess of healers, midwives, physicians, and all those who work to alleviate suffering and restore physical health, emotional and spiritual. She is the source of divine healing, the living water that quenches the soul's thirst and restores the vitality of the body.

The Crone, the third face of Brigid, represents the fire of poetic inspiration, the creative flame that awakens imagination, intuition, and artistic expression. She embodies wisdom, introspection, transformation, and connection with ancestral knowledge. Crone Brigid is the goddess of poets, bards, seers, sages, and all those who seek truth, beauty, and wisdom through art, poetry, and contemplation. She is the source of divine inspiration, the muse who whispers secrets to the ears of those who open themselves to her voice.

The attributes and symbols associated with Brigid reflect her triple and multifaceted nature. The sacred fire is, naturally, her central symbol, representing the flame of life in all its manifestations. Brigid's fire is not only physical fire, but also spiritual fire, the energy that animates creation, the passion that drives action, and the light that illuminates the path of the soul. Brigid's sacred fire is a symbol of purification, transformation, protection, inspiration, and connection with the divine.

The healing spring is another important symbol of Brigid, representing her capacity for healing and renewal. Sacred springs, wells, and rivers were places of worship for Brigid, considered portals to her healing and purifying energy. The water of Brigid's spring symbolizes emotional, physical, and spiritual healing, the ability to cleanse the wounds of the soul, restore the health of the body, and quench the soul's thirst for connection with the divine.

The lyre and the loom are symbols that represent Brigid's aspect as the goddess of poetry and artistic inspiration. The lyre symbolizes music, poetry, harmony, and the beauty of creative expression. The loom symbolizes the art of weaving, the creation of complex patterns from simple threads, representing Brigid's ability to weave the magic of word, image, and sound to inspire and transform. These symbols evoke the importance of the arts in Celtic spirituality and the ability of Brigid to awaken creativity and artistic expression in her devotees.

Brigid's domains encompass healing, protection, home, fertility, poetry, inspiration, childbirth, and feminine wisdom. She is invoked for the healing of physical, emotional, and spiritual illnesses, for the protection of home and family, for the fertility of the earth and the body, for creative inspiration in artistic projects, and for assistance during childbirth and motherhood. Brigid is a compassionate and accessible goddess, who cares about the well-being of all beings and who offers her help to those who seek her with a sincere heart.

The myths and stories associated with Brigid reveal her compassion, her healing power, and her divine inspiration. In many narratives, she appears as a skilled healer, using herbs, sacred waters, and her own energy to alleviate suffering and restore health. Her connection to childbirth and motherhood is evident in many traditions, being invoked as the protector of mothers and children. And her poetic inspiration is celebrated in legends that describe her as the muse of bards and poets, granting them the gift of word and eloquence.

Connecting with Brigid in rituals and devotional practices is to seek her healing, her protection, her inspiration, and her blessing for home and family. We can invoke Brigid when we need physical, emotional, or spiritual healing, when we seek protection for our home and loved ones, when we need inspiration for creative projects, or when we wish to strengthen our connection with the divine feminine energy. We can offer Brigid offerings that reflect her domains, such as white or red candles, sandalwood or rosemary incense, spring water, milk, bread, flowers, and handicrafts. We can meditate on her symbols, such as the fire, the spring, and the lyre, seeking her energy and inspiration. And we can honor her through acts of healing, compassion, creativity, and care for the home and the community.

In short, the figure of Brigid, with her intrinsic triplicity, presents herself not as a mere mythological construct of the past, but as a vibrant and perennial archetype, whose relevance echoes through the ages to the present. As we contemplate her facets of Maiden, Mother, and Crone, we unveil a multifaceted mirror of the human experience, reflecting the cycles of life, renewal, and accumulated wisdom. The Maiden embodies innate potential, the promise of new beginnings, and the flame that ignites in the home, symbolizing hope and domestic protection. The Mother manifests the vital force that heals and nourishes, representing compassion, care, and the regenerative capacity inherent in life itself. The Crone, finally, personifies deep wisdom, introspection, and poetic inspiration, inviting us to delve into the depths of ancestral knowledge and to express beauty and truth through art and contemplation. This triad, far from being fragmented, weaves a complex and harmonious tapestry, demonstrating the fundamental interconnection between the various aspects of existence and the feminine divinity. Brigid's energy, therefore, transcends mere adoration of a distant entity, inviting active and conscious participation in the primordial forces that shape our reality.

By internalizing the teachings and symbols associated with Brigid, we open a portal to the enrichment of our own journey. The sacred flame, the central symbol of her essence, invites us to cultivate passion and inspiration in all areas of our lives, igniting the fire of creativity and action. The healing spring reminds us of the importance of holistic well-being, the restoration of physical, emotional, and spiritual health, and the need to nurture our being in all dimensions. The lyre and the loom inspire us to embrace the beauty and harmony of artistic expression, to recognize the transformative power of word, music, and creativity in our journey of self-discovery and connection with the world. Invoking Brigid, therefore, is not limited to external rituals, but rather to an internal posture of openness to healing, compassion, inspiration, and protection in our homes and in our lives. It is to cultivate the flame of hope, to nourish the source of healing within us, and to weave the beauty of our own creative expression into the loom of existence.

Ultimately, Brigid emerges as a timeless archetype, whose message resonates with particular force in the contemporary world. In an era marked by fragmentation, by the relentless search for meaning, and by the urgent need for healing and renewal, her triplicity offers a model of integration and wholeness. She invites us to recognize the inherent sacredness of everyday life, to honor the cycles of life, to value ancestral wisdom, and to nurture our innate capacity for healing, creativity, and compassion. By connecting with Brigid's energy, whether through meditation, artistic practice, or acts of service and care, we open ourselves to an inexhaustible source of strength and inspiration, strengthening our bond with the sacred that resides in us and in the world around us. Thus, Brigid not only guides us in the search for healing, protection, and inspiration, but also invites us to awaken to our own divine nature, recognizing in ourselves the vital flame, the source of healing, and the spark of creativity that echo her triple and luminous essence.

Chapter 12
Cernunnos
God of Wild Nature

A translucent veil seems to separate the known world from the primordial realms, a threshold where perception transforms and the essence of nature reveals itself in its most genuine form. We have left behind the domains where the trifold flame radiated its wisdom, and we now venture along the enigmatic paths that wind through ancient forests and untouched landscapes. In this new horizon, where the air vibrates with a wild energy and the earth pulses with ancestral rhythms, we are called to unravel the mysteries of a deity shrouded in shadows and legends, a being whose influence extends to every corner of untamed nature. Prepare to meet Cernunnos, the guardian of the deep forests, the lord of wild animals, the very personification of the life force that emanates from untouched nature. Within the Celtic pantheon, he stands as an imposing figure, his domains encompassing vast forests, rugged mountains, and all the beings that inhabit them. Cernunnos manifests as the indomitable energy that flows in rushing rivers and verdant valleys, the primary force that governs the cycles of life and death, abundance, and the perpetual renewal of nature. His presence is felt in the bellow of the stag, the silent flight of the owl, the whisper of the wind among the ancient trees, a wild symphony that echoes through the ages.

To delve into the understanding of Cernunnos is to embark on a journey to the deepest roots of our connection with the natural world. He presents himself as a guide for those who seek the ancestral wisdom of the forest, the protection of wild creatures, and revitalization through the incessant cycles of nature. Upon contemplating Cernunnos, we are invited to recognize the inherent sacredness of the natural world, to revere its rhythms and mysteries, and to find in its essence the key to our own vitality and renewal. He reminds us of our interdependence with the web of life, of our role as an integral part of a complex and interconnected system, and of the importance of honoring and protecting the wild force that resides both externally and within the core of our being.

Cernunnos, in his essence, represents the primordial force of wild nature, the vital energy that pulses in untouched forests, towering mountains, and rushing rivers. He is the personification of the indomitable power of nature, the raw and beautiful force that exists beyond human control, reminding us of our deep interdependence with the natural world. Cernunnos invites us to recognize the sacredness of nature, to respect its rhythms and cycles, and to find our own strength and vitality in connection with the wild world.

As the "Lord of Animals," Cernunnos rules over all wild creatures, from the majestic stags and bears to the smallest birds and insects. He is the guardian of the herds, the protector of wild animals, the master of the hunt, and the provider of abundance for those who depend on nature for their sustenance. Cernunnos teaches us respect for animals, to recognize their instinctive wisdom, and to understand our place within the web of life, not as dominators, but as an integral part of an interconnected ecosystem.

Cernunnos is also deeply associated with fertility, abundance, and the cycle of life and death. His horned image, with its antlers, symbolizes virility, reproductive power, and connection with the rhythms of nature. He is the god of material prosperity, of the bounty of harvests, of the abundance of the hunt, and of the fertility of the earth. Cernunnos reminds us of the cyclical nature of life, of the perpetual dance between birth, growth, decline, and rebirth, and of the promise of renewal and abundance that always arises after periods of darkness and scarcity.

The attributes and symbols associated with Cernunnos reflect his wild, fertile, and cyclical nature. The antlers are undoubtedly his most iconic symbol, representing his connection to the animal world, his virility, his strength, and his link to the cycles of nature. The antlers, which fall off and grow back each year, symbolize renewal, rebirth, and the cyclical nature of life. They also represent the connection with animal instinct, the wisdom of nature, and the ability to adapt and thrive in wild environments.

The serpent is another animal frequently associated with Cernunnos, representing his connection to the earth, to the underground mysteries, and to the kundalini energy, the life force that resides at the base of the spine. The serpent symbolizes earthly wisdom, healing, transformation, and connection to the cycles of renewal and regeneration. It also represents the primordial energy of life, the life force that winds through nature and manifests itself in all life forms.

The torc, a rigid metal necklace, is a human symbol often associated with Cernunnos, representing his nobility, his leadership, and his authority as lord of wild nature. The torc symbolizes power, royalty, and connection with the civilized human world. The presence of the torc in representations of Cernunnos may indicate the bridge between the wild world and the human world, or the idea that even wild nature has its own form of nobility and intrinsic order.

Wild animals in general, such as stags, bears, wolves, and bulls, are important symbols of Cernunnos, representing his connection to the animal kingdom, his protection of wild creatures, and his connection to the life force of nature. Wild animals symbolize freedom, independence, instinctive strength, and natural wisdom. The presence of animals around Cernunnos in his representations emphasizes his role as guardian and lord of the animal kingdom.

The domains of Cernunnos encompass forests, wild animals, hunting, the fertility of the earth, the cycle of nature, and material prosperity. He is invoked for protection in the forests, for abundance in hunting, for the fertility of the earth and herds, for connection with the animal world, and for the pursuit of prosperity and abundance. Cernunnos is a generous and protective god, who offers his help to those who seek him with respect and reverence for nature.

The myths and stories associated with Cernunnos, although less abundant compared to other Celtic deities, reveal his deep connection with nature and his role as lord of the wild world. His image appears in various artistic representations of the Celtic era, often associated with hunting scenes, fertility rituals, and representations of exuberant nature. His iconography suggests a widespread and popular cult, linked to rural life, hunting, agriculture, and reverence for nature. Although written myths are scarce, his iconographic presence and his persistence in the folklore of various Celtic regions attest to his importance and enduring power.

Connecting with Cernunnos in rituals and devotional practices is to seek his protection in wild nature, his blessing of fertility and abundance, and his ancestral wisdom of the earth. We can invoke Cernunnos when we venture into nature, to ask for protection and guidance in forests, mountains, and other wild places. We can ask for his help to increase the fertility of the earth, to ensure good harvests, to attract material prosperity, and to strengthen our connection with the cycle of nature. We can offer Cernunnos offerings that reflect his wild and earthly nature, such as tree branches, animal feathers, forest herbs, grains, fruits, red wine, or mead. We can meditate on his symbols, such as the antlers, the serpent, and the wild animals, seeking his energy and inspiration. And we can honor him by spending time in nature, connecting with forests, rivers, mountains, and animal life, recognizing the sacredness of the natural world and our place within it.

In a world increasingly distant from natural rhythms, the figure of Cernunnos resurfaces not only as a relic of an ancestral past but as a beacon illuminating the way back to the essence of life. His message transcends the centuries, echoing through concrete forests and asphalt deserts, reminding us that, even in the most urbanized corners, wild nature persists, both in the outside world and within the innermost being of each individual. By internalizing the teachings of Cernunnos, we are impelled to question our role on the planet, to reconsider our relationship with other species, and to re-evaluate the values that guide our existence. In a time when speed and technology often disconnect us from the tangible and the essential, Cernunnos invites us to slow down, to observe, to feel the earth beneath our feet and the breeze on our face, to reconnect with the vital cycle that sustains us and of which we are an inseparable part.

The reverence for Cernunnos, therefore, is not just a mere cult of an ancient deity, but a profound recognition of the interconnection of all life and the vital importance of preserving the wild force that resides at the heart of nature. It is a call to action, an invitation to become guardians of the forests, defenders of animals, and protectors of the fertility of the earth. By honoring Cernunnos, we also honor our own essential nature, our capacity to feel, to love, to create, and to marvel at the beauty and mystery of the natural world. In this sense, connecting with Cernunnos is to embark on a journey of personal and collective transformation, towards a more harmonious and sustainable future, where humanity and nature can coexist in balance and mutual respect.

Thus, as we conclude this immersion in the universe of Cernunnos, we take with us his horned image, the strength of wild animals, the mystery of the serpent, and the nobility of the torc, not as mere archetypal symbols, but as guides for a continuous journey of rediscovery and reconnection. May the energy of Cernunnos inspire us to tread wilder paths, to honor the rhythms of nature in our lives, and to passionately defend the sacredness of the natural world, so that future generations can also hear the bellow of the stag, the whisper of the wind in the trees, and feel the vital pulse of Mother Earth.

Chapter 13
Danu
The Mother Goddess, Source of Life

In a universe where energies intertwine in cosmic dances, guided by the ancestral compass of knowledge, we are now led to contemplate the primary essence that emanates from the very fabric of existence. After exploring the vigorous and untamed manifestations of a divinity connected to the cycles of wild nature, our journey takes us to an even deeper portal: the threshold of primordial creation. Let us prepare to enter the mystery that resides in the original source, in the cosmic womb from which everything emerges, the driving force behind the web of life, the ancestral matrix that pulses at the heart of being. This is the moment to turn our gaze to the fundamental principle, the root of all manifestation, seeking to understand the inaugural energy that gave rise to the cosmos and everything that inhabits it.

This force, venerated in immemorial times by various cultures under multiple names and archetypes, manifests itself in the Celtic pantheon under the majestic figure of Danu, the primordial Mother Goddess. Recognized as the divine ancestor of the Tuatha Dé Danann, Danu is not merely a deity among others, but rather the very personification of cosmic motherhood, the inexhaustible source of all life. She is the primordial abundance that pours from the ether, the universal nourishment that sustains creation, and the generative power that ignited the spark of existence. As we approach Danu, we are connecting with the very matrix of life, unraveling the secrets of the original source, seeking a guide for those who yearn for sustenance, for flourishing, for maternal support, and, above all, for a deep connection with the first origins.

Unveiling Danu is, therefore, more than knowing a deity; it is embarking on an odyssey towards understanding the matrix of existence. It is diving into the primordial waters from which all life emanates, seeking the ancestral wisdom that resides in the very source. It is treading a path that will lead us to essential nourishment, to the fertility that resides in every atom of being, to the unconditional protection of the Great Mother, and to the intrinsic connection with the origin of all things. This is the invitation that presents itself: to enter the realm of Danu, the Mother Goddess, Source of Life, and allow her primordial energy to guide us towards a deeper understanding of ourselves and the universe around us.

Danu, in her essence, represents the very source of life. She is the primordial Mother Goddess, the one who gave birth to the Celtic pantheon, the Tuatha Dé Danann, and who, in many traditions, is considered the mother of all gods and all creatures. Her energy is the energy of creation, of generation, of the feminine principle that gives shape and substance to the universe.

Danu is the matrix of existence, the cosmic womb from which all life emanates, and the nurturing force that sustains and nourishes creation at all its levels. She invites us to recognize the sacredness of life, to honor our own origin, and to connect with the primordial source of all existence.

As Mother Goddess, Danu represents motherhood in its purest and most comprehensive form. Her motherhood transcends the idea of biological motherhood, encompassing the nurturing, care, protection, and unconditional love that extends to all creation. She is the cosmic mother who nourishes and sustains all beings, offering shelter, comfort, and protection to her sons and daughters at all times of life. Danu teaches us the value of maternal care, the importance of physical and spiritual nourishment, and the strength of unconditional love that heals, protects, and strengthens.

Danu is also deeply associated with primordial abundance. She is the source of plenty, prosperity, and wealth that emanates from nature itself. Her energy is present in the fertile earth that produces abundant harvests, in the waters that irrigate and nourish life, and in the generosity of nature that offers its gifts to all beings. Danu invites us to recognize the abundance inherent in the universe, to open our hearts to receive the gifts of life, and to cultivate gratitude for the plenty that surrounds us.

The attributes and symbols associated with Danu reflect her maternal, primordial, and abundant nature. The fertile earth is, naturally, one of her most important symbols, representing her ability to generate life, nurture creation, and offer sustenance to all beings. The fertile earth symbolizes the abundance of nature, the promise of bountiful harvests, the security of home, and the solid foundation upon which life manifests. It also represents nourishment, stability, and connection with the deep roots of existence.

The primordial water is another essential symbol of Danu, representing the source of life, the matrix of creation, and the constant flow of vital energy that permeates the universe. Primordial water symbolizes purity, fluidity, healing, emotion, and connection with the unconscious. It also represents the source of all creation, the cosmic amniotic fluid from which all life emerges.

The abundance of nature in general, manifested in flowers, fruits, plants, and lush landscapes, is a recurring symbol of Danu, representing her generosity, her plenty, and the beauty that emanates from her maternal energy. The abundance of nature symbolizes prosperity, plenty, beauty, harmony, and the full manifestation of life in all its forms. It also represents divine generosity, the gift of life, and the promise that needs will always be met.

Danu's domains encompass creation, fertility, nourishment, motherhood, and the abundance of the earth. She is invoked for fertility in relationships, projects, and life in general, for physical, emotional, and spiritual nourishment, for maternal protection, for assistance in motherhood, and to attract abundance and prosperity into life. Danu is an accessible and compassionate goddess, who welcomes all who seek her with an open heart and who offers her nourishment and maternal protection to all her sons and daughters.

The myths and stories associated with Danu, although less narrative and more focused on her primordial function, reveal her fundamental importance in the Celtic pantheon. Her very designation as "mother of the gods" already attests to her central position and her reverence as the source of all Celtic divinity. In many traditions, her name is linked to the rivers Danube, Dnieper, and Don, emphasizing her connection with primordial waters and the life force that flows through the earth. Although specific myths about her actions and adventures are less prominent, her presence permeates Celtic cosmology as the fundamental force of creation, nourishment, and life.

Connecting with Danu in rituals and devotional practices is to seek her maternal nourishment, her blessing of fertility and abundance, and her protection as primordial mother. We can invoke Danu when we need physical, emotional, or spiritual nourishment, when we seek fertility in projects and relationships, when we need maternal protection and support in times of difficulty, or when we wish to connect with the primordial source of life. We can offer Danu offerings that reflect her maternal and abundant nature, such as milk, honey, bread, fruits, flowers, seeds, and pure spring water. We can meditate on her symbols, such as the fertile earth, the primordial water, and the exuberant nature, seeking her energy and inspiration. And we can honor her through acts of care for the earth, for nature, for other living beings, and for ourselves, recognizing the sacredness of life and the maternal nourishment that sustains us all.

Danu's domains extend far beyond the verdant fields of ancient Ireland, resonating through time to our day as a primordial archetype of feminine power and life force. As we contemplate the intricate tapestry of her symbols and attributes, we are invited to recognize the presence of the Mother Goddess not only as a distant mythological figure, but as a living and pulsating energy that permeates the very essence of existence. Danu personifies the promise of constant renewal, the endless cycle of birth, growth, death, and rebirth that sustains the cosmos. She reminds us that, even in the darkest moments, the seed of life remains latent, awaiting the right conditions to germinate and flourish again. Her nurturing and protective energy offers a safe haven in times of uncertainty, a constant reminder that we are never truly alone, for we carry within us the divine spark of creation, the primordial echo of Danu's cosmic womb. Thus, by honoring Danu, we are not only revering an ancestral deity, but awakening in ourselves the awareness of our own intrinsic connection with the source of life, with the inexhaustible abundance that resides in the heart of nature, and with the infinite potential for flourishing that resides in every being.

The invocation of Danu in rituals and devotional practice represents a deep dive into the primordial waters of our own psyche, an invitation to reconnect with our deepest roots and to nourish our being on all levels. By offering Danu the symbols of her essence – the nourishing milk, the golden honey, the comforting bread, the succulent fruits, the vibrant flowers, the promising seeds, and the pure spring water – we are establishing a sacred dialogue with the Mother Goddess, expressing our gratitude for her generosity and opening our hearts to receive her blessings. Meditation on her archetypal symbols, such as the fertile earth that pulsates with life, the primordial water that flows incessantly, and the exuberant nature that manifests itself in all its glory, allows us to tune into Danu's vibrational frequency, absorbing her nourishing and inspiring energy. Honoring Danu through acts of care for the earth, for nature, and for all living beings reflects our commitment to cultivating the sacredness of life in all its forms, recognizing that we are all sons and daughters of the Great Mother, interconnected by the invisible web of creation.

Ultimately, Danu's message transcends the boundaries of time and culture, echoing through the centuries as a beacon of hope and renewal for humanity. In a world often marked by fragmentation, disconnection, and the incessant search for external validation, Danu invites us to turn our gaze inward, to the inexhaustible source of wisdom and love that resides in each of us. She reminds us that true abundance does not reside in the accumulation of material goods, but in the ability to cultivate gratitude for the gifts of life, in the generosity of sharing our gifts with the world, and in the deep connection with the web of life that unites us to all beings. By embracing Danu's principles – nourishment, protection, fertility, and abundance – we can tread a path of healing and transformation, both on a personal and collective level, building a more harmonious and sustainable future for ourselves and for generations to come, honoring the sacredness of life in every breath and recognizing the presence of the Mother Goddess in every beat of our hearts.

Chapter 14
Gods and Goddesses of Nature

Emerging from the depths of the primordial matrix, the journey to understand the forces that weave reality expands to horizons of splendor and complexity. After contemplating the generating energy, we are now led to a domain of even vaster manifestations: the vibrant realm of the deities that animate the world. Not isolated entities, but rather emanations of a cosmic consciousness that expresses itself in the myriad of forms and energies that constitute existence. This is an invitation to unravel the intricate web of power that pulses at the heart of nature, a dive into the subtle currents that connect the visible and the invisible, the earthly and the ethereal. Let us prepare to explore a universe of divine archetypes, each radiating a unique facet of the life force that permeates all things, an interconnected system where every element, however small, plays a crucial role in the cosmic dance of creation.

In this intricate system, the deities of nature stand out, beings of light and power who personify the primordial energies that shape the tangible world. These are not ethereal and distant figures, but rather living and pulsating presences that inhabit the elements that surround us. Rivers and lakes gain voice through aquatic gods, mountains rise in majesty as a reflection of celestial entities, forests whisper ancestral secrets under the protection of sylvan goddesses, winds and storms manifest divine fury and renewal, and the seasons dance in a perpetual cycle orchestrated by cosmic forces. To understand these deities is to delve into the essence of nature itself, to recognize the immanent intelligence that resides in each element, and to decipher the sacred codes inscribed in the landscape that surrounds us.

As we examine this natural pantheon, we are invited to transcend the utilitarian view of the world and awaken to the intrinsic sacredness that resides in every manifestation of life. Recognizing the divine presence in the rivers that nourish the earth, in the mountains that challenge the sky, in the forests that harbor mysteries, in the winds that announce changes, and in the seasons that rhythm existence, is to cultivate a relationship of deep reverence for the web of life that sustains us. It is to awaken to the awareness that we are an integral part of a larger system, interconnected by invisible threads to all forms of life, and responsible for honoring and preserving the harmony of this delicate balance. This is the path to reconnect humanity with the primordial source of all existence, to rediscover the sacred in everyday life, and to nurture a deep sense of belonging and responsibility towards the planet that shelters us.

In the Celtic worldview, nature was not merely a passive setting or a resource to be exploited, but rather a living, conscious realm full of divine forces. Every natural element, from the humblest wildflower to the most imposing mountain, was imbued with spirit, vital energy, and the presence of the gods. The ancient Celts perceived the divine not as something distant and transcendent, but as something immanent, present in every manifestation of nature, pulsing in the rhythm of the seasons, in the flow of waters, in the breath of the winds, and in the life force of the earth. This animistic view of the world, this belief in the soul of the world, permeated all aspects of Celtic life, from ritual practices to social organization and artistic expression.

Within this vast panorama of nature deities, we find a myriad of beings of power and beauty, each governing a specific domain of the natural world. Gods of rivers and lakes personified the fluidity of waters, healing, purification, and connection to the underworld. Goddesses of springs and fountains were revered as sources of life, fertility, and poetic inspiration. Mountain gods personified strength, stability, protection, and connection to the celestial realms. Forest goddesses were guardians of wildlife, protectors of animals, and personifications of the ancestral wisdom of nature. Gods of winds and storms manifested the transformative power of atmospheric forces, change, renewal, and vital energy in constant motion. And deities of the seasons personified the perpetual cycles of nature, the rhythm of life, death, and rebirth, and the cosmic dance of time.

Among the water deities, we find figures like Flidais, an Irish goddess associated with deer, the forest, and, in some traditions, with water. Although primarily linked to wild nature and animals, her connection to water sources can be interpreted as a manifestation of the divinity that nourishes and sustains life through pure and invigorating waters. Belisama, a goddess revered in Gaul, was associated with lakes and rivers, and her name, which means "the brightest" or "the strongest," evokes the brightness and strength of clear waters. Thermal springs dedicated to Belisama were places of healing and purification, reflecting the therapeutic and spiritual power of the waters under her domain. These are just a few examples of the myriad of aquatic deities who were revered by the Celts, each with their attributes and local legends, but all sharing the fundamental connection with the vital and mysterious force of water.

Mountains, with their imposing presence and solidity, were also considered the dwellings of powerful deities. Although specific names of mountain gods are less prominent in written sources, the veneration of mountains as sacred places and the belief in mountain spirits were central elements of Celtic spirituality. Mountain heights were seen as portals to other worlds, meeting places between heaven and earth, and sources of ancestral power and wisdom. Cernunnos himself, with his antlers that rise like mountain peaks, can be interpreted as a deity who embodies the strength and majesty of mountains, in addition to his domains over wild nature and animals.

Forests, dense and mysterious, were the quintessential realm of wild nature for the Celts, and they housed a variety of deities and spirits. Artio, a bear goddess revered in the region of Bern, Switzerland, personified the strength, protection, and instinctive nature of bears, animals that inhabited the forests and were symbols of power and bravery. Tree spirits, the Dryads, and forest spirits, the Fauns, were also an integral part of the Celtic spiritual landscape, considered guardians of the forest, protectors of wildlife, and manifestations of the living soul of nature. Forests were seen as natural temples, places of mystery, magic, and encounter with the divine immanent in nature.

Winds, invisible and powerful forces, were also personified by deities. Although specific names of wind gods are less frequent, the belief in the power of the winds as messengers of the gods, as forces of change and renewal, was present in Celtic spirituality. The winds could be invoked to bring good news, to ward off negative energies, to assist in journeys, and to manifest the transformative power of change and renewal. Storms, with their overwhelming force, were also seen as manifestations of divine power, reminding us of the dual and dynamic nature of nature's energy.

The seasons, with their cycles of birth, growth, decline, and rebirth, were personified by deities who governed the rhythms of nature and influenced the fertility of the earth and the lives of agricultural communities. Although the specific names of seasonal deities vary in different modern Celtic traditions, the celebration of the seasonal festivals of the Celtic Wheel of the Year, such as Samhain, Imbolc, Beltane, and Lughnasadh, demonstrates the profound reverence for the cycles of nature and the belief in divine influence on the changes of the seasons. These festivals were times of connection with the deities of nature, of celebration of life, death, and rebirth, and of harmonization with cosmic rhythms.

Honoring the Gods and Goddesses of Nature is a fundamental aspect of Celtic spiritual practice. Recognizing the divine immanent in nature, respecting the spirits of places, giving thanks for the gifts of the earth, and seeking harmony with natural rhythms are essential practices for the Celtic disciple. Outdoor rituals, in natural places such as forests, rivers, lakes, and mountains, are powerful ways to connect with these deities. Simple offerings, such as flowers, herbs, grains, pure water, or small handmade objects, can be offered in natural places as a form of gratitude and reverence. Meditation in natural landscapes, mindful walking in the forest, attentive observation of the cycles of the moon and the seasons, and the simple act of spending time in contact with nature, seeking the divine presence in every detail, are devotional practices that strengthen our connection with the Gods and Goddesses of Nature.

In the modern world, often distanced from nature and immersed in a frenetic and artificial pace of life, reconnection with the Gods and Goddesses of Nature becomes even more important. To reclaim this animistic view of the world, to relearn how to listen to the voice of nature, to respect its rhythms and cycles, and to recognize the divine presence in every living being, can bring us healing, balance, and a deep sense of belonging to the web of life. Honoring the Gods and Goddesses of Nature is honoring ourselves as an integral part of nature, it is recognizing our interdependence with the planet, and it is treading a path of respect, reverence, and responsibility towards the natural world that sustains us.

In our present day, as humanity increasingly distances itself from natural rhythms and the subtle forces that sustain life, the call of the nature deities resounds as an invitation to reconnect with the sacred. This call does not require blind devotion or inflexible dogmas, but rather an awakening to the interconnectedness between all beings and elements of the living world. Listening to the wind whispering through the trees, feeling the pulsating energy of the waters, recognizing the solidity of the mountains, and perceiving the cyclical dance of the seasons is to remember that nature is not separate from us — we are part of it, and therefore responsible for its preservation and balance.

Those who choose to honor these ancient gods and goddesses, whether through outdoor rituals, symbolic offerings, or simple contemplation of the landscape, are resuming an ancestral practice that strengthens the harmony between the human and the divine. Every river, forest, mountain, or breeze carries the memory of eras in which spirituality was intertwined with everyday life, and to reclaim this perception is to open oneself to a more connected, intuitive, and meaningful existence. The relationship with the forces of nature does not need to be complex or distant — it manifests itself in respect for natural cycles, in the recognition of subtle signs, and in the commitment to the earth that nourishes us.

Thus, as we look to the future, the path is drawn not as a nostalgic return to the past, but as a fusion between ancestral knowledge and contemporary consciousness. Integrating this sacred vision of the world into modern life can be the first step to restore lost balance and cultivate an authentic spirituality, rooted in the earth and the energies that flow through it. If each individual can recognize their connection to the web of life, honoring the gods of nature not only with words, but with actions of respect and care, then the legacy of these ancient forces will remain alive, flowing like the eternal waters that feed the heart of the world.

Chapter 15
Spirits and Ancestors

Here ends the exploration of the abode of the primordial deities, the stage where elemental forces gain form and personality. However, the Celtic cosmic tapestry extends far beyond this familiar domain, unveiling a universe replete with ethereal presences and enigmatic entities. Let us prepare to transcend the limits of the main pantheon, venturing into realms less visible, yet equally vibrant, where a myriad of spiritual beings weave the fabric of existence. This is an invitation to peer into the depths of Celtic cosmology, unveiling the multifaceted layers that make up its spiritual reality.

In this vast and intricate web, we recognize that palpable reality is only a fraction of the total spectrum. Invisible dimensions pulsate with a life of their own, inhabited by entities that transcend conventional human understanding. They are not to be confused with the supreme deities, but are distinct spiritual beings, each imbued with their own domains, traits, and purposes within the Celtic cosmic order. Interaction with these entities is not an exception, but rather an integral part of the experience of existence, demanding wisdom and reverence to preserve balance and harmony between the human plane and the spiritual realm.

Among the myriad of "Other Beings" that populate this expansive sphere, the Spirits of Nature stand out, entities intrinsically connected to specific locations in the natural world. Considered guardians of their domains, manifestations of the vital essence of nature, and links between humanity and the divine, these beings play multifaceted roles in Celtic cosmology. Further on, we will explore the central concept of the Sidhe and the ancestral practice of Veneration, delving into the nuances of interaction with these spiritual presences that shape the rich tapestry of the Celtic world.

In the Celtic worldview, reality was not limited to the tangible physical plane, but extended to invisible dimensions, populated by beings of different natures and levels of consciousness. These beings were not necessarily gods in the full sense, but rather spiritual entities with their own domains, characteristics, and purposes, playing important roles in the dynamics of the Celtic cosmos. Interaction with these beings was seen as a natural part of life, and respect and wisdom were essential to maintain balance and harmony in the relationships between the human world and the spiritual world.

Among the most prominent "Other Beings," we find the Spirits of Nature, entities intrinsically linked to specific natural locations, such as trees, rivers, stones, mountains, and springs. These spirits, often called fairies, elves, gnomes, or earth spirits in different traditions and regions, were considered guardians of their natural domains, manifestations of the living soul of nature, and intermediaries between the human world and the divine world. Their nature was ambiguous, and they could be both beneficial and malicious, depending on how they were treated and the intention of those who sought their interaction.

The concept of Sidhe (pronounced "Shee") occupies a central place in the understanding of nature spirits in the Celtic tradition, particularly in Ireland and Scotland. The Sidhe, also known as the "Fairy Folk" or "Gentle People," is a comprehensive term that refers to a variety of spiritual beings who inhabit the Celtic Otherworld, a realm parallel to our physical reality, interpenetrated with the natural world. The Sidhe are described as beautiful, powerful, and magical beings, with abilities that transcend the laws of physics as we know them. They can appear in various forms, from luminous and ethereal human figures to fantastic and elemental creatures.

The Sidhe's relationship with the Otherworld is intrinsic. It is believed that the Sidhe reside in Sidhe mounds, ancient earth mounds, hills, and other natural locations that were considered portals to the Otherworld. These locations were seen as sacred and special, charged with magical energy and connected to the spiritual realms. It was believed that, at certain times of the year, especially during seasonal festivals like Samhain and Beltane, the veil between the worlds became thinner, facilitating passage and interaction between the human world and the world of the Sidhe.

The Sidhe, although they could be enchanting and offer gifts and assistance, were also feared and respected, as their nature could be capricious and their actions unpredictable. Disrespecting the Sidhe, invading their domains without permission, or offending their sensibilities could attract negative consequences, such as illness, misfortune, or even abduction to the Otherworld. On the other hand, treating the Sidhe with respect, offering gifts, and honoring their customs could bring good luck, protection, healing, and magical aid. Interaction with the Sidhe, therefore, required caution, etiquette, and a deep understanding of their nature and their domains.

Beyond nature spirits and the Sidhe, Ancestral Veneration was a fundamental pillar of Celtic spirituality. The ancestors were seen not as figures of the distant and forgotten past, but as living and active presences in the spiritual world, capable of influencing the lives of their descendants and the community. It was believed that the ancestors remained connected to the world of the living, offering protection, guidance, wisdom, and spiritual assistance. Honoring the ancestors was, therefore, an essential practice to maintain family and community balance, to strengthen ties with the past, and to ensure the continuity of lineage and traditions.

Ancestral veneration in the Celtic tradition was not limited only to direct family ancestors, but also extended to mythical ancestral figures, heroes, tribal leaders, and earth spirits who were considered the founders and protectors of the community and territory. Locations such as ancestral tombs, earth mounds, memorial stones, and places of historical significance were revered as points of contact with the ancestors, places where one could seek their guidance and blessing. Rituals, offerings, prayers, and the telling of ancestral stories were common practices to keep alive the connection with the past and honor the memory of those who came before.

Interaction with nature spirits and ancestors, in the Celtic tradition, required a balanced and respectful approach. It was not about dominating or controlling these entities, but rather establishing relationships of reciprocity, honor, and mutual respect. Offering gifts, showing gratitude, following local customs, asking permission before entering their domains, and acting with sincere intention were key elements for a positive and harmonious interaction. Seeking help and guidance from nature spirits and ancestors was seen as legitimate and beneficial, as long as it was done with ethics, responsibility, and respect for the differences between the human world and the spiritual world.

It is important to emphasize that the Celtic spiritual world was not populated only by benevolent and friendly beings. As in physical nature, there were forces and entities that could be challenging, dangerous, or even malicious. Celtic wisdom recognized the duality inherent in existence, the presence of light and shadow on all planes, and the importance of discerning and protecting oneself from negative energies and hostile entities. Protection rituals, amulets, prayers, and seeking guidance from protective deities were important practices to ensure safety and well-being on the spiritual journey.

For the modern Celtic disciple, understanding and honoring the "Other Beings" of the Celtic world is to enrich their spiritual practice, expanding their vision of reality and deepening their connection with the web of life. Recognizing the presence of nature spirits in natural places, honoring the memory of ancestors, and cultivating a respectful relationship with the spiritual world are important steps on the disciple's journey. It is not about seeking contact with these entities lightly or out of mere curiosity, but rather cultivating a deep reverence for the sacredness of life in all its manifestations and seeking harmony and balance in the relationships between the human world and the spiritual world.

As we delve into the universe of Celtic spirits and ancestors, we understand that the connection with these beings is not just a rescue of the past, but an experience that transcends time and continues to manifest in the present. Respect for the subtle forces of nature and reverence for ancestors are pillars of a spirituality that is not limited to worship, but that is expressed in attitudes, in everyday rites, and in the way one inhabits the world. Every grove, every spring, and every sacred mound carries living memories of those who came before, whispering teachings to those who know how to listen.

The journey through the Celtic spiritual world is an invitation to expanded perception, to sensitivity to the signs that the invisible interweaves into the fabric of reality. The spirits of nature and the Sidhe walk among us, framing the landscape with their intangible presence, sometimes protective, sometimes challenging. The ancestors, in turn, remain as guides, inspiring strength and wisdom to those who keep the flame of remembrance burning. Between silent offerings and prayers whispered to the wind, the connection with these beings is strengthened, not as a search for power or dominion, but as a pact of respect and reciprocity.

Thus, when treading the paths of the Celtic tradition, the modern disciple encounters an essential truth: the sacred is in everything, pulsating in the earth under one's feet and in the stars above one's head. Honoring spirits and ancestors is, above all, recognizing this sacredness inherent in existence and integrating it into one's own life. In the harmony between worlds, between times, and between beings, lies the key to an authentic, vibrant spirituality deeply rooted in the web of life.

Chapter 16
Understanding Celtic Rituals

The time has come to enter an essential realm of ancient Celtic wisdom, a nerve center that emanates energy and meaning. After a journey through the divine figures, the entities of nature, and the myriads of spirits that populate the Celtic universe, we now glimpse the core of their spiritual practice. Let us not dwell on the surface of mere formal repetitions or beliefs devoid of vigor; let us prepare to recognize instruments of profound reach, keys that open doors to unexplored dimensions of existence.

These means, far from being relics of a remote past, represent active pathways to establish a genuine connection with the sacred that resides in all things. Through them, it is possible to tune into the symphony of nature, orchestrating a harmony between the inner and the outer. More than that, they offer the promise of metamorphosis, an alchemical process that transmutes personal experience and propels the celebration of life in each of its manifestations. To unlock the latent potential in these practices, it is essential to penetrate their intrinsic logic, to grasp the philosophy that gives them substance and purpose.

Understanding the rationale and essence of these ceremonies is the foundation for authentic and conscious participation. Instead of limiting ourselves to the execution of external gestures, we are invited to immerse ourselves in the primordial intention that animates them, to embrace sincerity as a guide, and to open ourselves to harvesting the benefits that manifest along the spiritual journey. These acts, which we will soon identify by their specific nomenclature, are more than words or movements; they are portals to experience, to transformation, and to deep connection with the forces that shape reality.

In their essence, Celtic rituals are intentional and symbolic acts that aim to establish a bridge between the human world and the spiritual world. They are a form of communication with the gods and goddesses, with the spirits of nature, with the ancestors, and with the subtle forces that permeate the universe. Through rituals, the practitioner seeks to leave ordinary time and space, enter a sacred space, and come into direct contact with the energies and entities of the spiritual world. Celtic rituals are, therefore, portals to other dimensions of reality, paths to the direct experience of the sacred, and tools for personal transformation and connection with the divine.

One of the primary purposes of Celtic rituals is connection with the gods and goddesses. The rituals offer a dedicated space and time to honor, invoke, and communicate with the deities of the Celtic pantheon. Through prayers, chants, invocations, offerings, and other ritual practices, the practitioner seeks to establish a personal relationship with the gods, seeking their guidance, protection, blessings, and assistance in different aspects of life. Rituals of devotion to the Celtic gods are expressions of faith, gratitude, and reverence, strengthening the bond between the human world and the divine world and cultivating a relationship of reciprocity and mutual respect.

Another fundamental purpose of Celtic rituals is harmonization with nature. Celtic spirituality, as we have explored previously, is deeply connected with the natural world, recognizing the intrinsic sacredness of nature and the divine presence in every element of the world around us. Celtic rituals are often performed in sacred natural places, such as forests, springs, rivers, mountains, and earth mounds, seeking to attune the practitioner to the energies of nature, the cycles of the seasons, and the spirits of the places. Rituals of harmonization with nature aim to restore the balance between human beings and the environment, cultivate respect for the web of life, and strengthen the connection with the wisdom and power of primordial nature.

Personal transformation is also a central objective of Celtic rituals. Through rituals, the practitioner seeks to promote positive changes in their life, overcome challenges, heal emotional and spiritual wounds, strengthen virtues, develop self-knowledge, and accelerate their spiritual growth. Rituals of personal transformation use symbols, archetypes, visualizations, energies, and spiritual entities to catalyze internal processes of change, break limiting patterns, release energetic blockages, and awaken the inner potential of each individual. Celtic rituals offer a path to healing, renewal, and the evolution of the soul, leading the practitioner to a more authentic, complete, and fulfilled version of themselves.

Healing, both physical, emotional, and spiritual, is an important purpose of many Celtic rituals. Believing in the interconnection between body, mind, and spirit, and in the influence of spiritual energies on health, Celtic healing rituals aim to restore energetic balance, strengthen the immune system, alleviate suffering, promote recovery, and awaken the self-healing power inherent in every human being. Healing rituals can involve the use of herbs, crystals, holy water, healing sounds, visualizations, invocations to healing gods and spirits, and the channeling of healing energies to the body, mind, and soul of the practitioner or others in need of assistance.

Celebration is also an essential aspect of Celtic rituals. Rituals are moments of joy, gratitude, community, and connection with the sacred in all its manifestations. The seasonal festivals of the Celtic Wheel of the Year, such as Samhain, Beltane, Imbolc, and Lughnasadh, are ritual celebrations that mark the cycles of nature, honor the gods and goddesses, celebrate the fertility of the earth and life, and strengthen community bonds. Celtic celebration rituals are moments of dance, music, chants, banquets, games, and other expressions of joy and communion, cultivating a sense of belonging, gratitude, and celebration of the gift of life.

The philosophy behind Celtic rituals is based on a few fundamental principles. Reciprocity with the gods is a key concept. It is believed that the relationship with the deities is a two-way street, where the devotion and offerings of the practitioner are reciprocated with the blessings, protection, and assistance of the gods. Celtic rituals are, therefore, acts of exchange and reciprocity, where the practitioner offers something of value (energy, time, intention, material offerings) in exchange for divine gifts and assistance. This reciprocity strengthens the bond between the human and the divine, cultivating a relationship of trust and mutual interdependence.

Intention and heart are essential elements in any Celtic ritual. It is believed that the effectiveness of a ritual depends not only on the words spoken or the gestures performed, but on the sincere intention and open heart of the practitioner. A ritual performed with clear intention, focus, and genuine emotion has much greater power than a ritual performed mechanically or superficially. Intention is the driving force behind the ritual, the energy that directs the action and attracts the spiritual energies and entities to the sacred space. The open heart, in turn, allows divine grace to flow freely through the practitioner, enhancing transformation and spiritual connection.

The dance between the visible and invisible worlds is another fundamental characteristic of Celtic ritual philosophy. Rituals are seen as moments when the veil between the worlds becomes thinner, allowing interaction and communication between the physical world and the spiritual dimensions. Celtic rituals recognize the interpenetration of visible and invisible reality, the constant presence of the spiritual world in our everyday world, and the possibility of accessing these other dimensions through specific ritual practices. This dance between the worlds is the essence of Celtic magic, the ability to influence reality through interaction with the energies and entities of the spiritual world.

The key elements of a Celtic ritual include the creation of a sacred space, through purification, consecration, and the casting of a magic circle. Invocations to the gods, spirits, and elements are fundamental to inviting the desired energies and entities to the ritual. Offerings are acts of reciprocity and gratitude, offering something of value to the spiritual beings. Dance, music, and chants raise the energy of the ritual, alter the state of consciousness, and facilitate connection with the sacred. Prayers and visualizations direct the intention of the ritual and focus the energy for the desired purpose. And the celebration concludes the ritual in an atmosphere of joy, gratitude, and communion.

It is important to emphasize that Celtic rituals are not rigid and immutable formulas, but rather flexible guidelines that can and should be adapted to the individual needs, intentions, and inspirations of each practitioner. Authenticity and personal connection with the ritual are more important than strict adherence to a predefined format. The Celtic disciple is encouraged to study the ritual traditions, to learn the fundamental principles, but also to trust their intuition, to adapt the rituals to their own needs, and to create ritual practices that resonate with their soul and their personal connection with the sacred.

Celtic ritual practice is not merely a set of repetitive actions, but a living and dynamic act, where intention and connection are the true conductors of the spiritual experience. Each ceremony is a link between times and worlds, a thread that intertwines the practitioner with the divine, the spirits, and the very essence of existence. Thus, rather than seeking to reproduce ancestral gestures, it is essential to understand the underlying logic of these rites and allow each one to resonate in its deepest meaning. When performed with sincerity and purpose, rituals become portals to self-knowledge, harmony with nature, and the manifestation of the sacred in everyday life.

By adopting this view, the modern disciple realizes that the true power of rituals does not reside in their structure, but in the ability to create a sacred space, where time bends and the veil between the worlds dissolves. Whether honoring the gods, seeking guidance from the ancestors, or celebrating the natural cycles, each ritual is an opportunity to renew the bond with the great web of life. Thus, it is not just about following pre-established steps, but about feeling and allowing the spirit of tradition to guide the gestures, words, and thoughts in a unique dance between past and present.

In the end, understanding Celtic rituals is accepting that they are more than external ceremonies — they are expressions of a living spirituality, which pulsates through nature, the seasons, and the human heart itself. The journey through ritual knowledge does not end with the memorization of prayers or the execution of rites, but in the genuine experience of the sacred in each act performed. Thus, by treading this path with respect, authenticity, and surrender, the practitioner not only honors the ancient customs, but keeps them alive, allowing their essence to continue to vibrate through the generations.

Chapter 17
Creating Sacred Space

Understanding the essence of ancestral rituals, delving into their philosophy, and unveiling their purposes is only the threshold of a deeper journey. After theoretical contemplation, the pressing need for practical application emerges, the materialization of knowledge into action. It is at this crucial point that the next step is revealed, a natural and inevitable unfolding for anyone who yearns to experience the totality of devotional practice: the meticulous construction of a sacred space. This act, far from being a mere preparatory protocol, ascends to the condition of a central pillar, the foundation upon which the entire structure of magic is erected.

This space, conceived and established with intention and precision, transcends mere physical delimitation; it configures itself as a domain apart, an intersection between the tangible and ethereal dimensions. Imagine a stage, not in the theatrical sense, but cosmic, where the ordinary laws of reality give way to subtle and powerful dynamics. It is in this unique place that the veil between worlds becomes thinner, facilitating dialogue between the human being and the spiritual currents that permeate existence. It is not just about creating a receptacle, but forging a link, a point of convergence where intentions and energies can manifest in an amplified and directed way.

The importance of such a construction lies in its intrinsic capacity to offer more than just a place of practice; it provides an energetically charged environment, a sanctuary immune to the chaotic influences of the profane world. By establishing a sacred space, we erect a protective barrier, an invisible shield that safeguards the practitioner and directs the energy flow of the ritual. This space acts as a catalyst, intensifying concentration, sharpening intuition, and enhancing the effectiveness of each devotional gesture. It is within this carefully defined perimeter that communication with spiritual entities becomes clearer, deeper, and Celtic magic, in all its potential, finds its most fertile ground.

The need to create a sacred space in Celtic rituals derives from the belief in the existence of multiple dimensions of reality, inhabited by diverse energies and entities. When performing a ritual, the practitioner seeks to connect with these other dimensions, attract specific energies, and establish communication with spiritual beings. However, the spiritual world is not without challenges and unwanted energies. Creating a sacred space serves as a protective barrier, separating the ritual space from the profane world and establishing a safe and clean environment for magical and devotional practice.

The sacred space also functions as an energy focuser. By delimiting and consecrating a specific space for the ritual, we concentrate our intention, direct our energies, and create a point of convergence for the spiritual forces we wish to invoke. The sacred space acts as a lens, intensifying the power of the ritual and facilitating the manifestation of our purposes and intentions. Within the magic circle, energies are amplified, the mind quiets, and the connection with the sacred becomes deeper and more intense.

In addition to protection and focus, the sacred space in Celtic rituals symbolizes a world apart, a temporary realm where the laws of ordinary time and space are suspended, and where the rules of the spiritual world become predominant. By crossing the threshold of the magic circle, the practitioner leaves behind the concerns of the everyday world and enters a sacred territory, a place where the impossible becomes possible, where magic flourishes, and where the soul reconnects with its divine essence. The sacred space is, therefore, a symbolic recreation of the Celtic Otherworld, a portal to the realms of magic and transformation.

The creation of a sacred space in Celtic rituals generally involves three main steps: purification, consecration, and the casting of the magic circle. Although there are variations in practices and traditions, these three steps are fundamental to establishing an effective and safe ritual space.

Purification of the space is the first step, aiming to cleanse the place of negative, stagnant, or unwanted energies. Purification prepares the energetic ground for consecration and for the entry of the positive and divine energies that will be invoked in the ritual. There are several ways to purify a space in the Celtic context, the most common being the use of the elements of fire, water, air, and earth.

Fire, represented by the smoke of incense or sacred herbs (such as sage, rosemary, cedar, or juniper), is used to purify the air and the environment through smudging, an ancestral practice of fumigation. The smoke is directed throughout the space, visualizing the cleansing of dense and negative energies, and the opening of the place for the entry of positive and beneficial energies.

Water, preferably spring water, rainwater, or seawater, is used to sprinkle the space, symbolizing emotional and spiritual cleansing, purification of the soul, and renewal of energies. The water can be sprinkled with the hands, with a branch of herbs, or with a sprinkler, visualizing the water cleansing and purifying every corner of the sacred space.

Air, represented by the sound of bells, drums, rattles, or chants, is used to vibrate the space, dissipate stagnant energies, and raise the vibrational frequency of the place. The sound can be directed to the four corners of the space, visualizing the sound waves cleansing and harmonizing the environment.

Earth, represented by salt or consecrated earth, can be used to draw a circle on the ground, delimiting the sacred space and anchoring the energies of the ritual in the physical plane. The salt or earth can be spread in a circle with the hands or with a ritual instrument, visualizing the creation of a protective barrier and the connection of the space with the energies of the earth.

After purification, the next step is the consecration of the space, which aims to bless and dedicate the place to the sacred purposes of the ritual. Consecration invokes the divine presence, establishes the sacred intention of the space, and fills it with positive and beneficial energies. Consecration can be performed through prayers, invocations to Celtic gods and goddesses, visualizations of light and divine energy, and the use of consecrated essential oils or holy water.

During consecration, the practitioner can walk through the space, directing their intention and visualizing the divine light descending and filling the place, making it sacred and special. Consecration prayers can be recited, invoking the presence of the gods and goddesses, asking for their blessing and protection for the ritual. Essential oils such as sandalwood, frankincense, myrrh, or lavender, known for their spiritual and purifying properties, can be used to anoint the space, raising its vibration and consecrating it to divine purposes. Holy water, prepared with intention and prayers, can also be used to sprinkle the space during consecration.

The casting of the magic circle, the last step in creating the sacred space, is a powerful symbolic act that delimits the ritual space, establishing a boundary between the profane world and the sacred world. The magic circle is not just a physical line drawn on the ground, but an energetic barrier, a shield of protection, and a portal to other dimensions. The circle can be drawn physically with salt, rope, flowers, stones, or simply visualized energetically with the hands, a staff, or a ritual sword.

When casting the circle, the practitioner usually invokes the four elements (Earth, Air, Fire, and Water) and the cardinal directions (North, East, South, and West), asking for their protection, presence, and balance in the sacred space. Each element and cardinal direction is associated with specific qualities, energies, and directions, and their invocation creates a circle of protection and power around the ritual space. Invocations can be performed with words, gestures, visualizations, and the lighting of candles or incense representing each element and direction.

Within the sacred space, usually in the center of the circle or at a specific point, the altar is established. The altar is the focal point of the ritual, the place where offerings are placed, where ritual instruments are placed, and where the energy of the ritual is concentrated. The altar can be a table, a tree trunk, a flat stone, or any elevated surface that is suitable for the purposes of the ritual. The altar is decorated with symbols, personal objects, representations of the gods and goddesses, candles, incense, flowers, crystals, and other elements that resonate with the intention of the ritual and with the practitioner's personal connection to the sacred.

The creation of a sacred space is a personal and meaningful act, which should be performed with attention, respect, and sincere intention. There is no single or "correct" way to create a sacred space, and the practitioner is encouraged to adapt the practices and elements to their own needs, beliefs, and inspirations.

The most important thing is that the sacred space is created with an open heart, a focused mind, and the intention of establishing a place of power, protection, and connection with the divine.

Creating a sacred space is much more than a simple preparation for the ritual; it is an act that reflects the practitioner's commitment to their spiritual journey. By delimiting this space with respect and intention, a link is established between the visible and the invisible, between the everyday and the sacred. More than a barrier of protection, it is an invitation for ancestral energies and the gods to be present, for time to slow down, and for the spiritual world to intertwine with the material world. Every gesture, from the purification of the environment to the casting of the magic circle, is a step to immerse oneself in the tuning of the ritual, making each action charged with meaning and power.

The modern Celtic practitioner, by understanding this construction not only as a technical procedure, but as a true alchemy of intention and energy, realizes that the sacred space is not something external, but also internal. The circle drawn on the ground is a reflection of the circle drawn in the mind and heart, a symbol of the temporary separation from the profane world to enter a state of greater connection and presence. Thus, by erecting their space of practice, each individual not only honors the ancestral traditions, but continues a knowledge that is renewed with each generation, adapting to the needs and experiences of those who keep it alive.

In the end, the sacred space is not just a physical place or a set of pre-defined rituals, but an extension of the practitioner's own essence, a reflection of their devotion and attunement to the divine. Creating it is an act of magic in itself, a moment of alignment and preparation that influences the entire ritual experience. Whether in a clearing in the forest, in a special corner of the house, or just within one's own consciousness, what really matters is the intention and respect for the sacred. When done with truth and surrender, the sacred space becomes a living portal, where the boundaries between worlds dissipate, and the practitioner stands, finally, before the mystery and enchantment of existence.

Chapter 18
Steps on the Sacred Journey

At the core of every genuine devotional practice lies a flow, an intrinsic dance that guides the practitioner through a predefined path, towards a meeting point with the transcendent. After the meticulous creation and energization of the sacred space, the stage is finally set for the unfolding of the ceremony itself, the beating heart of Celtic connection. This crucial moment transcends mere formality; it inaugurates an initiatory journey, a dive into the depths of the soul and the subtle currents of energy that permeate existence. It is at this point that the boundaries between the ordinary world and the realm of the sacred begin to fade, paving the way for an immersive and transformative experience.

The unfolding of this ritual journey is not random, but rather orchestrated by an ancestral structure, a framework that serves as a map and compass for the explorer of the spirit. This structure, far from being a set of inflexible rules, resembles a mighty river that, although it has defined banks, allows for a graceful and adaptable fluidity to the terrain it crosses. Understanding this fundamental architecture is like deciphering an ancient code, a practical knowledge that empowers the individual to conduct their practices with focused intention, harmonious order, and an effectiveness that resonates in the deepest layers of being. By internalizing this sacred roadmap, the practitioner acquires the confidence necessary to navigate the intricacies of the ritual, moving with clear purpose towards the core of the devotional experience.

By embarking on this structured exploration, the disciple not only follows a protocol, but also aligns with an ancestral energetic pattern, a continuous cycle of opening, interaction, and withdrawal. This methodical progression, although outlined in distinct steps, is essentially a unified movement, a cosmic breath that begins with the invocation of the sacred and culminates in its graceful closure. It is through this ritual dance that the true tapestry of the Celtic experience is woven, leading the practitioner to an altered state of consciousness, a threshold where connection with the divine becomes not only possible, but palpable and deeply transformative.

It is important to emphasize that the structure of a Celtic ritual is not rigid or dogmatic, but rather a flexible model that can be adapted and customized according to the needs, intentions, and inspirations of each practitioner. Celtic traditions and lineages may present variations in the details and order of the steps, but the fundamental essence of the ritual structure remains the same: a circular and cyclical movement that begins with the opening of the sacred space and is completed with its closure, leading the practitioner to a transformative experience of connection with the divine.

The basic structure of a Celtic ritual can be understood in seven main steps, which interlink and complement each other in a harmonious energy flow:

Opening and Purification:

This initial step aims to mark the beginning of the ritual, declare the sacred intention of the practice, and reaffirm the creation of the sacred space as a place apart from the profane world. The opening can be performed in various ways, including:

Lighting of candles: Candles can be lit on the altar or at the cardinal points, symbolizing the flame of devotion, the light of consciousness, and the presence of the elements and directions in the sacred space.

Ringing of a bell or drum: The sound of a bell or drum can be used to mark the beginning of the ritual, call attention to the present moment, and raise the vibration of the space.

Declaration of Intention: The practitioner can verbalize or mentally state the intention of the ritual, clearly expressing the purpose of the devotional practice and directing the energy towards the desired goal.

Reaffirmation of Purification: One can reaffirm the purification of the space, visualizing the clean and vibrant energy that fills the magic circle, and reinforcing the intention to create a safe and sacred place.

Invocation of the Elements and Directions:

After the opening, the next step is the invocation of the four elements (Earth, Air, Fire, and Water) and the cardinal directions (North, East, South, and West). This act aims to invite the elemental and directional energies into the sacred space, seeking their balance, protection, and beneficial influence on the ritual. The invocation can be performed in various ways:

Verbal Invocation: Recitation of specific prayers or invocations for each element and direction, expressing their qualities, attributes, and asking for their presence and assistance.

Ritual Gestures: Performing symbolic gestures with the hands, body, or ritual instruments (wand, athame, etc.) directed towards each cardinal point, visualizing the manifestation of the elemental energies.

Lighting of Elemental Candles or Incense: Candles or incense of colors and scents associated with each element can be lit and directed towards the respective cardinal points, intensifying the invocation and connection with the elemental energies.

Visualization: Visualization of the energies of the elements and directions flowing into the sacred space, filling it with their qualities and power.

Invocation of the Deities:

With the elements and directions invoked, the next crucial step is the invocation of the Celtic deities who are the main focus of the ritual. This act aims to invite the gods and goddesses into the sacred space, seeking their presence, guidance, blessing, and direct interaction in the ritual. The invocation of the deities can be performed in various ways:

Formal Verbal Invocation: Recitation of traditional prayers, hymns, or invocations dedicated to the chosen deities, expressing their attributes, myths, and asking for their manifestation in the ritual.

Intuitive Call: A more personal and spontaneous call, coming from the heart of the practitioner, expressing their desire for connection with the deities and their longing for their presence and assistance.

Chants and Music: Chants, mantras, or devotional music dedicated to the deities can be sung or played, raising the vibration of the space and facilitating communication with the divine.

Visualization of the Divine Presence: Visualization of the deities manifesting in the sacred space, feeling their energy, their presence, and their response to the call.

Magical Work and Devotion:

After the invocation of the deities, the center of the ritual is dedicated to magical work and devotion itself. This is the time to carry out the main intention of the ritual, whether for healing, protection, abundance, personal transformation, gratitude, or any other specific purpose. The activities performed in this step can vary widely depending on the nature of the ritual and the practitioner's preference, including:

Prayers and Chants: Recitation of personal or traditional prayers, devotional chants, mantras, or words of power directed to the deities or the purpose of the ritual.

Meditation and Visualization: Guided or spontaneous meditative practices, creative visualizations, shamanic journeys, or other techniques to alter the state of consciousness and connect with energies and spiritual entities.

Energy Manipulation: Techniques of directing and manipulating energy (such as visualization, breathing, movement, sound) to channel vital force for the purpose of the ritual, whether for healing, protection, manifestation, or transformation.

Specific Rituals: Performing specific rituals for the desired purpose, such as healing rituals with herbs and water, abundance rituals with offerings and seeds, protection rituals with amulets and enchantments, or divination rituals with oracles and intuition.

Offerings: Presentation of offerings to the gods, spirits, or ancestors, as a form of reciprocity, gratitude, and honor. Offerings can be material (food, drinks, flowers, incense, handcrafted objects) or energetic (time, personal energy, devotion, prayers).

Thanksgiving and Blessings:

After the magical work and devotion, it is essential to express thanks and gratitude to the deities, spirits, elements, and directions that were invoked and participated in the ritual. This step acknowledges the collaboration of the spiritual world, strengthens the bonds of reciprocity, and closes the ritual interaction in a respectful and harmonious way. Gratitude can be expressed through:

Words of Gratitude: Verbalization or mentalization of sincere words of thanks to the deities, spirits, elements, and directions, recognizing their presence, help, and blessings.

Gestures of Reverence: Performing gestures of reverence, such as bowing the head, bowing down, or raising the hands in a sign of gratitude and respect.

Closing Offerings: Burning incense of gratitude, a final offering of flowers, or other symbolic objects as a form of gratitude and closure of the ritual exchange.

Blessings: Asking and receiving blessings from the gods, elements, and directions for self, beloved ones and to the world, expanding the ritual's positive energy beyond the sacred space.

Farewell to the Deities and Elements:

After thanksgiving, the next step is the farewell to the deities, spirits, elements, and directions that were invoked. This act formally ends the ritual communication, releasing the energies and entities to return to their own planes of existence, and undoing the energetic bond established during the ritual. The farewell should be performed with respect and gratitude, recognizing the presence and assistance of the spiritual entities, and releasing them with appreciation and consideration. The farewell can be performed through:

Words of Farewell: Recitation of farewell phrases, thanking the deities, spirits, elements, and directions for their presence and assistance, and releasing them to depart in peace.

Gestures of Release: Performing symbolic gestures with the hands or ritual instruments to release the energies and entities, undoing the energetic bond and allowing them to return to their own realms.

Extinguishing Elemental Candles or Incense: Extinguishing the candles or incense that represented the elements and directions, symbolizing their departure and the return of the elemental energies to their natural state.

Closing and Grounding:

The last step of the ritual is the closing and grounding. The closing formally ends the ritual, undoing the magic circle and reintegrating the practitioner into the ordinary world. Grounding aims to reconnect the practitioner with the earth's energy, dissipate excess ritual energy, and facilitate the return to the state of everyday consciousness in a balanced and harmonious way. Closing and grounding can be performed through:

Opening the Magic Circle: Symbolically undoing the magic circle, opening the energetic portal and allowing the sacred space to return to its natural state. This can be done by undoing the circle drawn on the ground, undoing the energetic visualizations, or performing ritual gestures of opening.

Thanks to the Location: Expressing gratitude to the place where the ritual was performed, whether it is a natural space, a home altar, or any other chosen location, recognizing its support and energy for the ritual practice.

Energetic Grounding: Performing energetic grounding techniques, such as touching bare feet on the ground, visualizing roots of energy connecting to the earth, eating something, or drinking water, to dissipate excess ritual energy and return to a state of physical and energetic balance.

Journaling the Ritual (Optional): Recording the experiences, insights, and results of the ritual in a magical diary or notebook, for later reflection and monitoring of spiritual progress.

By understanding and experiencing each of these steps, the practitioner not only follows a tradition but becomes part of it, allowing the energy of Celtic rituals to flow in an authentic and meaningful way. Ritual practice, more than a sequence of acts, is a living language, a form of dialogue between the human and the divine, between the visible and the invisible. Every gesture, word, and intention reverberates in the subtle planes, strengthening the bonds with ancestral spirits and with the forces of nature that permeate existence.

When performed with devotion and awareness, the Celtic ritual transcends mere symbolic repetition and becomes a bridge to the sacred, a vehicle for personal and spiritual transformation. With each new practice, the practitioner deepens their connection with the mysteries of the tradition, adjusting and refining their own energetic attunement. This path is not a fixed destination, but a journey in constant evolution, where each experience shapes understanding and strengthens communion with natural cycles and deities.

The Celtic ritual structure reminds us of the cyclical nature of life, where each beginning carries within it the seed of closure, and each end prepares the ground for a new beginning. By closing the circle and returning to the everyday world, the practitioner carries with them not only the energy of the ritual, but also the wisdom and blessings gathered in this encounter with the sacred. Thus, the journey continues, intertwining the threads of time and spirituality in an eternal dance of connection and renewal.

Chapter 19
Celtic Invocation and Prayers

Understanding the essence of Celtic spirituality is like deciphering an ancestral code, where language manifests as the master key to the invisible realms. In the pulsating heart of the Celtic tradition, there is a deep recognition that the universe resonates with an interconnected web of energies, where the physical and spiritual worlds dance in harmony. Within this vibrant worldview, spoken word and silent intention intertwine, forming ethereal bridges that connect the practitioner to the cosmic fabric. The search for connection with the sacred, therefore, is not a passive journey, but rather an active dialogue, an energetic exchange that manifests through specific forms of ritualistic communication. It is in this liminal space, between the tangible and the ethereal, that invocation and prayer emerge as primordial tools, acting as the very language of the sacred within the Celtic ritual structure.

At the core of Celtic ritual practice, invocation and prayer transcend mere repetition of words; they are configured as acts of profound energetic and communicative significance. Imagine them as conducting wires, capable of transporting the practitioner's intention, desire, and devotion towards the spiritual planes. Invocation, with its character of calling and invitation, opens portals of communication with deities, nature spirits, and venerated ancestors. Prayer, more intimate and personal, is configured as a direct dialogue with the divine, an expression of the soul that seeks comfort, guidance, or simply the joy of connection. Both, in their essence, represent the human capacity to reach and interact with the invisible forces that permeate reality, establishing an essential channel of communication for the Celtic spiritual experience.

The journey towards mastery of Celtic invocation and prayer is, therefore, a quest to refine the ability to dialogue with the sacred. By deepening the understanding and practice of these arts, the practitioner not only enriches their ritual experience, but also strengthens the intrinsic relationship with the divine. This process of communicative refinement is fundamental to unlocking deeper layers of spiritual connection, allowing the ancestral wisdom and vital energy of the Celtic world to flow freely through ritual practice. By delving into the study of invocation and prayer, we prepare to explore the language that transcends the ordinary, paving the way for a deeper and more transformative sacred experience.

Invocation, in a Celtic ritual, is the act of calling, inviting, and crying out for the presence of a specific deity, a nature spirit, a venerated ancestor, or an elemental force. Invocation is not merely reciting words, but rather an act of deep intention, concentration, and energetic projection, aiming to establish a direct and conscious connection with the desired spiritual entity.

An effective invocation resonates with the energy of the invoked entity, vibrating in tune with its essence and opening a channel of communication between the human and spiritual worlds.

Invocation, in a Celtic ritual, is the act of calling, inviting, and crying out for the presence of a specific deity, a nature spirit, a venerated ancestor, or an elemental force. Invocation is not merely reciting words, but rather an act of deep intention, concentration, and energetic projection, aiming to establish a direct and conscious connection with the desired spiritual entity. An effective invocation resonates with the energy of the invoked entity, vibrating in tune with its essence and opening a channel of communication between the human and spiritual worlds.

The purpose of invocation in a Celtic ritual can vary depending on the practitioner's intention and the nature of the ritual. In devotional rituals, the invocation aims to honor and celebrate the deity, express gratitude, seek their blessing, and strengthen the personal relationship. In magical rituals, the invocation may aim to request assistance, guidance, power, or intervention from the deity to achieve a specific purpose, such as healing, protection, abundance, or personal transformation. In rituals of connection with nature, the invocation may be directed to the spirits of places, elementals, or forces of nature, seeking harmonization, balance, and communication with the natural world.

Prayer, in the Celtic ritual context, is a more personal and intimate form of communication with the sacred. While invocation has a more formal and ceremonial character, prayer is a direct expression of the heart, a dialogue of the soul with the divine. Celtic prayers can take various forms, from pleas and requests for help to declarations of love, gratitude, and praise. Prayer is an act of surrender, of opening the heart, and of recognizing the divine presence in our lives and in the world.

Celtic prayers can be spontaneous, improvised at the time of the ritual, or they can be traditional prayers, transmitted orally or written in ancient or contemporary texts. Spontaneous prayers carry the authenticity and emotion of the present moment, expressing directly and personally the feelings and longings of the practitioner. Traditional prayers connect the practitioner with the Celtic spiritual lineage, with ancestral wisdom, and with the power of words that have been repeated by generations of devotees. The choice between spontaneous or traditional prayers, or a combination of both, depends on the practitioner's personal preference and the nature of the ritual.

The language used in Celtic invocation and prayers is an important element to consider. Although there is no specific "sacred language" in the modern Celtic tradition, the choice of words, the rhythm of speech, and vocal intonation can influence the effectiveness of ritual communication. Many modern practitioners use English or the local language in their invocations and prayers, seeking authenticity and direct understanding of the words spoken. Others may choose to include words or phrases in ancient Celtic languages (such as Old Irish, Scottish Gaelic, or Welsh), seeking a deeper connection with the ancestral roots of the tradition.

Regardless of the chosen language, the language of Celtic invocations and prayers tends to be poetic, evocative, and rich in imagery. Metaphors, similes, personifications, and allusions to the myths, attributes, and symbols of Celtic deities are often used to enrich the ritual expression and awaken the practitioner's imagination and emotion. Celtic ritual language seeks to transcend rational and linear communication, appealing to intuition, sensitivity, and direct connection with the sacred.

The formula of a Celtic invocation or prayer may vary, but generally includes some common elements:

Greeting and Recognition: Beginning with a respectful greeting to the invoked deity, spirit, or force of nature, recognizing their name, epithets, and attributes. Example: "O Dagda, Good God, Father of All, Lord of Abundance and Wisdom, I greet you and welcome you to this sacred space."

Declaration of Intention: Clear expression of the purpose of the invocation or prayer, stating the reason for the call, the desire for connection, the request for help, or the expression of gratitude. Example: "I invoke your presence in this ritual to seek your guidance on my journey, to receive your protection against challenges, and to celebrate the abundance that you grant to my life."

Appeal to Attributes and Domains: Reference to the attributes, domains, myths, and symbols of the invoked deity, seeking to resonate with their specific energy and awaken the desired qualities in the practitioner. Example: "Dagda, with your inexhaustible cauldron, nourish my soul with your generosity; with your powerful club, protect me from all evil; with your magical harp, inspire my wisdom and creativity."

Request or Plea (Optional): Clear and respectful formulation of the specific request or plea, if the purpose of the invocation is to seek divine help or intervention. Example: "I ask for your help, O Dagda, to find solutions to the challenges that arise in my path, to overcome obstacles, and to manifest abundance in my life."

Promise of Devotion and Reciprocity: Expression of the practitioner's devotion, their commitment to the deity, and their intention to honor them and reciprocate their blessings. Example: "In gratitude for your presence and help, O Dagda, I promise to honor your name, follow your teachings, and share the abundance I receive with those in need."

Thanksgiving and Release: Closing of the invocation or prayer with words of thanks, blessing, and release of the deity or spirit, recognizing their presence and allowing them to return to their own plane of existence. Example: "I deeply thank you for your presence and generosity, O Dagda. May your blessing remain with me and with this sacred space. Depart in peace, and may our connection remain strong and alive."

The practice of Celtic invocation and prayer involves not only the recitation of words, but also the body posture, breathing, visualization, and emotional state of the practitioner. Upright posture, conscious breathing, visualization of the invoked deity or spirit, and a state of open and receptive heart can intensify the effectiveness of the invocation and prayer, facilitating communication with the sacred. Repetition, regularity, and sincerity in the practice of Celtic invocation and prayer deepen the relationship with the divine, refining the language of the soul and opening the doors to the grace and wisdom of the gods and spirits.

Mastering the art of invocation and prayer within Celtic spirituality is more than memorizing words or reciting fixed formulas; it is about tuning into the vibration of the sacred and allowing the energy to flow authentically. Each invocation, each prayer, becomes an echo of the soul that resonates through time and space, uniting past and present in a single melody of devotion. As the practitioner delves deeper into this ancestral language, they discover that true communication with the divine does not require perfection, but rather truth, intention, and a heart open to mystery.

Continuous practice strengthens the bond with spiritual forces, creating a cycle of reciprocity where the sacred not only listens, but also responds. Whether through subtle signs of nature, intuitive insights, or the simple feeling of presence and welcome, divine responses manifest in unexpected ways, reinforcing the connection between the visible and invisible worlds. Thus, invoking a deity or chanting a prayer is not just an act of faith, but a commitment to listening and interaction, where spirituality ceases to be something distant and becomes a living and transformative experience.

By integrating invocations and prayers into their journey, the practitioner builds a unique path, guided by ancestral wisdom and shaped by their own essence. Over time, the words become an extension of the soul, and communication with the divine becomes as natural as breathing itself. In this way, the Celtic tradition lives on, renewing itself with each voice that dares to call, with each heart that opens to the sacred, and with each step taken in the eternal dance between the human and the divine.

Chapter 20
Celtic Prayers
Models and Inspiration

In times immemorial, the search for connection with the transcendent has always permeated the human journey. In various cultures and spiritual traditions, the need arises to establish direct communication with the sacred, expressed through specific forms of language. Within the realm of Celtic spirituality, this search manifests itself in a particular and profound way, revealing an intricate system of dialogue with the forces of nature and ancestral deities. Celtic invocations and prayers thus represent a vital link, a means by which one seeks to express devotion, ask for help, and honor the entities that inhabit the sphere of the sacred.

To deepen the understanding of this sacred language and make it accessible to individual experience, it is essential to contemplate concrete manifestations of this devotional exchange. The presentation of practical examples of invocations and prayers directed to entities revered in the Celtic pantheon offers a valuable resource. Such examples are not limited to mere illustrations; they function as luminous guides, reference points that illuminate the path to the creation of an authentic and personal devotional practice. Through the analysis of these models, it becomes possible to discern the essential elements, the underlying structure, and the essence that animates communication with the divine in the Celtic context.

It is fundamental, however, to internalize that such examples represent only the starting point in an intrinsically personal and unique journey. The soul of Celtic spirituality resides in its inherent adaptability and in the freedom granted to each individual to shape their own devotional expression. The beauty of this path lies in the possibility of modifying, expanding, and recreating the invocations and prayers, imbuing them with one's own voice, intention, and emotion. The primary objective is to allow the words to emanate genuinely from the heart, laden with sincerity and feeling, thus establishing a true and deep connection with the Celtic sacred.

It is important to remember that these examples are only suggestions, and the beauty of Celtic spirituality lies in its flexibility and adaptability. Feel free to modify, adapt, and expand these invocations and prayers, using them as a guide to create your own unique and authentic devotional expressions. The most important thing is that your words come from the heart, laden with sincere intention and genuine emotion.

Example 1: Invocation to Dagda, "The Good God, the Father of All" (For Abundance, Protection, and Wisdom)

Greeting: O Dagda, Good God, Father of All, Lord of Abundance and Wisdom, guardian of the inexhaustible cauldron and the mighty club, I greet you and welcome you to this sacred space.

Intention: I invoke your presence in this ritual to seek your blessing of abundance in my life, your protection against all evil, and your wisdom to guide my steps on the path of the journey.

Appeal to Attributes: Dagda, with your cauldron of plenty, nourish my life with prosperity and sustenance. With your protective club, ward off negative energies and obstacles from me. With your magic harp, awaken in me ancestral wisdom and divine inspiration.

Request: I ask for your help, O Dagda, so that abundance may flow freely in all areas of my life, so that I may be protected from all danger, and so that your wisdom may illuminate my decisions and choices.

Devotion: In gratitude for your generosity and protection, O Dagda, I promise to honor your name, practice sharing and generosity, and seek wisdom in all my actions.

Thanksgiving and Release: I deeply thank you for your presence and blessings, O Dagda. May your plenty, protection, and wisdom remain with me and with this sacred space. Depart in peace, and may our connection remain strong and alive. So be it!*

Example 2: Prayer to the Morrigan, "The Goddess of War, Fate, and Sovereignty" (For Courage, Transformation, and Autonomy)

Greeting: Morrigan, Warrior Goddess, Lady of Fate and Sovereignty, raven-shaped, force of battle, and weaver of the wyrd, I greet you and honor your presence in this sacred circle.

Intention: In prayer, I seek your strength to face life's challenges, your guidance to understand my destiny, and your inspiration to claim my inner sovereignty.

Appeal to Attributes: Morrigan, with your warrior fury, grant me the courage to overcome obstacles and fight for what I believe in. With your prophetic vision, reveal to me the paths of destiny and help me discern the choices that are presented. With your indomitable sovereignty, inspire me to govern my own life with strength and integrity.

Request: I ask, O Morrigan, that you grant me the bravery to face my shadows and fears, the clarity to understand my life purpose, and the autonomy to follow my own path with confidence and determination.

Devotion: In reverence for your transformative power, Morrigan, I promise to honor my inner truth, act with courage and justice, and seek sovereignty over my own soul.

Thanksgiving and Release: I deeply thank you for your presence and strength, Morrigan. May your courage, wisdom, and sovereignty remain with me and guide me on my journey. Depart in peace, and may our connection remain strong and alive. So be it!*

Example 3: Invocation to Brigid, "The Triple Goddess of Fire, Healing, and Poetry" (For Healing, Inspiration, and Protection of the Home)

Greeting: Brigid, Triple Goddess of Fire, Healing, and Poetry, flame of the hearth, source of healing, and muse of inspiration, I greet you and welcome your sacred light into this space.

Intention: I invoke your presence to bring healing to my body, mind, and spirit, to awaken creative inspiration in my soul, and to protect my home and my loved ones with your sacred fire.

Appeal to Attributes: Brigid Maiden, Mother, and Crone, with the fire of the hearth, warm and protect my home. With the waters of healing, restore my health and well-being. With the flame of poetry, awaken my creativity and inspiration.

Request: I ask, O Brigid, that your healing may flow through me, restoring my health and vitality. May your inspiration guide me in my creative projects, and may your protective fire surround my home and my family, warding off all evil.

Devotion: In devotion to your triple nature, Brigid, I promise to honor the sacred fire, practice healing and compassion, and cultivate beauty and inspiration in my life.

Thanksgiving and Release: I deeply thank you for your presence and blessings, Brigid. May your healing, inspiration, and protection remain with me and radiate throughout my home. Depart in peace, and may our connection remain strong and alive. So be it!*

Example 4: Prayer to Cernunnos, "The Lord of Animals, God of Wild Nature" (For Connection with Nature, Abundance, and Strength)

Greeting: Cernunnos, Lord of Animals, God of Wild Nature, horned and powerful, guardian of the forests and master of the hunt, I greet you and honor your ancestral presence in this sacred place.

Intention: In prayer, I seek your guidance to connect with the wisdom of nature, your blessing of abundance and prosperity, and your strength to tread the wild path of life.

Appeal to Attributes: Cernunnos, with your antlers of a stag, connect me with the rhythm of nature and the cycle of life. With your connection to wild animals, teach me instinctive wisdom and harmony with the natural world. With your abundance of the forest, grant me plenty and prosperity.

Request: I ask, O Cernunnos, that you guide me in the forests of life, that you grant me the wisdom of animals, that you bless me with the abundance of nature, and that you strengthen my connection with the earth and with the cycle of life and death.

Devotion: In reverence for your wild and abundant nature, Cernunnos, I promise to honor the earth and animals, practice sustainability, and live in harmony with the rhythms of nature.

Thanksgiving and Release: I deeply thank you for your presence and guidance, Cernunnos. May your strength, abundance, and wisdom of nature remain with me and sustain me on my journey. Depart in peace, and may our connection remain strong and alive. So be it!*

Example 5: Invocation to Danu, "The Mother Goddess, Source of Life" (For Nourishment, Fertility, and Primordial Connection)

Greeting: Danu, Primordial Mother Goddess, Source of Life, matrix of all creation and universal nurturer, I greet you and celebrate your sacred presence in this circle.

Intention: I invoke your maternal energy to nourish my body, mind, and spirit, to awaken fertility in my projects and relationships, and to connect me with the primordial source of all life.

Appeal to Attributes: Danu, with the fertile earth, nourish me with the abundance of life. With the primordial waters, purify me and renew me. With your maternal love, protect me and support me at all times.

Request: I ask, O Danu, that your nourishment may flow through me, strengthening my health and vitality. May your fertility manifest in my projects and relationships, and may your maternal love surround me and protect me on all paths.

Devotion: In devotion to your cosmic motherhood, Danu, I promise to honor life in all its forms, practice care and nurturing, and recognize your presence in all things.

Thanksgiving and Release: I deeply thank you for your presence and nourishment, Danu. May your maternal love, fertility, and abundance remain with me and radiate to all creation. Depart in peace, and may our connection remain strong and alive. So be it!*

These are just a few examples to inspire your own journey in creating Celtic invocations and prayers. Explore the attributes, myths, and symbols of each deity, tune in to your own intuition and emotion, and allow the words to flow from your heart. Constant practice and experimentation are the keys to developing a personal and powerful sacred language, capable of weaving your own tapestry of connection with the Celtic divine.

As you explore these invocations and prayers, you realize that each word uttered carries the weight of devotion, the sincere call of the heart in search of connection with the sacred. More than simple ritualistic formulas, these prayers are living expressions of Celtic spirituality, reflecting the deep relationship between the practitioner and the divine forces. With each invocation, a bridge is built between the visible and the invisible, allowing the energy of the gods, spirits, and ancestors to manifest in a tangible and meaningful way.

The beauty of this path lies in the freedom of adaptation, in the fusion of tradition and personal intuition. Each practitioner, by shaping their own words and intentions, not only honors the ancients but also continues a sacred legacy that transcends time. Thus, invocation and prayer become acts of creation, where the inner voice echoes through the veils of the spiritual world, strengthening bonds, receiving blessings, and deepening communion with the Celtic divine.

May these inspirations serve as guides, but may the true power be born from the genuine feeling of each practitioner. For it is in authenticity, in sincere devotion, and in the opening of the heart that the magic of words manifests, transforming simple prayers into doorways to the sacred. May the journey continue, guided by the breath of the ancestors and the living flame of Celtic spirituality, always renewed by the voice of those who dare to call.

Chapter 21
Celtic Offerings to Gods and Spirits

It is in the interstices of the fabric of reality, where the veil between worlds becomes thinner, that the essence of genuine communication flourishes. If at the threshold of our exploration, we unveiled the intricacies of invocation and prayer – words as ethereal bridges cast to the realm of the Celtic sacred – now, we are led to enter a complementary domain, where language transcends the verbal and manifests in concrete acts of giving. Let us prepare to unveil the mysteries that permeate offerings, ancestral gestures laden with symbolism and intention, which echo through the ages as primordial expressions of our relationship with the invisible forces that shape existence.

The act of offering. More than a simple gift, within this gesture resides a universe of profound meanings. In Celtic ritual traditions, the offering manifests as a tangible link between the devotee and the divine, a cosmic dance of reciprocity where human generosity finds echo in spiritual abundance. These are not mere "payments" or attempts to bargain with the deities, but rather acts imbued with reverence, gratitude, and a deep desire to nurture and strengthen the bonds that unite us with the spiritual world. By demystifying the nuances of the practice of offerings, we shed light on the intricate web of relationships that underpin the Celtic worldview, understanding that the path to the sacred is not made only with words, but also with the universal language of giving.

In this new ritualistic horizon that unfolds, we will delve into understanding the multifaceted purpose of Celtic offerings. We will explore how these acts of surrender transcend mere materiality, becoming vehicles of devotion, instruments for strengthening bonds, and expressions of the search for blessings. We will unveil how to honor and harmonize with the spirits that inhabit nature and the ancestors who preceded us, finding in offerings a means to express respect, peaceful coexistence, and gratitude for the myriad gifts that the spiritual world grants us. By embracing the ancestral wisdom of offerings, we enrich our spiritual journey, deepening the connection with the sacred and solidifying the foundations of a reciprocal and harmonious relationship with the spiritual entities we revere.

Offerings, in Celtic rituals, are not mere "payments" or attempts to "bribe" the deities or spirits to obtain favors. Instead, they are understood as gifts, demonstrations of appreciation and respect, and acts of reciprocity within a sacred relationship. The philosophy of Celtic offerings is based on the idea that the relationship with the spiritual world is a mutual exchange, a dance of giving and receiving, where human generosity is matched by divine generosity.

The main purpose of Celtic offerings can be understood in several aspects:

Expressing Devotion and Gratitude: Offerings are a tangible way of expressing our love, respect, and devotion to the gods and goddesses, nature spirits, and ancestors. They are gestures that demonstrate our reverence and appreciation for their blessings, assistance, and presence in our lives. The act of offering is, in itself, a declaration of recognition of their importance and power.

Strengthening the Bond and Reciprocity: By offering gifts, we establish and strengthen the bond of reciprocity with the spiritual world. Offerings symbolize our commitment to maintaining a balanced relationship of mutual exchange, where we give and receive in equal measure. It is expected that human generosity will be answered with divine generosity in the form of blessings and aid.

Seeking Blessings and Favors: In some rituals, offerings may be offered with the intention of requesting specific blessings, assistance in challenges, or the manifestation of desires. In these cases, the offering serves as a respectful request, demonstrating the sincerity of the intention and the value of what is sought in return. It is important to note that this purpose should not be the only or main one, but rather an extension of the relationship of reciprocity and devotion.

Honoring and Appeasing Spirits: Offerings can also be used to honor nature spirits, spirits of places, or ancestors, seeking to appease them, obtain their permission to perform a ritual in their domain, or simply demonstrate respect and harmonious coexistence. In this context, offerings can be seen as "courtesy gifts" to maintain good relations with the surrounding spiritual world.

The types of Celtic offerings can vary widely, reflecting the diversity of gods, spirits, and ritual intentions. Both in antiquity and in modern Celtic practice, offerings can be categorized into several types:

Offerings of Food and Drink: These are the most common and traditional offerings, symbolizing sustenance, nourishment, and sharing the bounty of the earth.

Solid Foods: Bread, cakes, fruits, grains, nuts, herbs, edible flowers, honey, cheese, meat (in some traditions, historically). The choice of food may be seasonal or associated with the deity or spirit being honored.

Drinks: Pure water, milk, mead, wine, beer, cider, fruit juices, herbal tea. Fermented alcoholic beverages, such as mead and beer, were particularly valued in the ancient Celtic tradition.

Offerings of Incense and Aromatics: The fragrant smoke of incense is seen as a vehicle to carry intentions and prayers to the spiritual world, in addition to purifying and elevating the vibration of the ritual space.

Resins: Frankincense, myrrh, benzoin, copal, dragon's blood (red resin).

Dried Herbs: Sage, rosemary, cedar, juniper, lavender, mugwort, verbena, according to the ritual intention and the deity honored.

Essential Oils: Can be used in diffusers or oil burners, or to anoint candles and other ritual objects.

Offerings of Art and Crafts: Handmade objects, which demonstrate time, dedication, and personal talent, are valuable offerings, representing human creativity and the effort dedicated to the sacred.

Drawings, Paintings, Sculptures: Artistic creations that represent the deity, the spirit, nature, or the intention of the ritual.

Poems, Music, Songs: Original compositions created in honor of the sacred.

Handcrafted Objects: Textiles, embroidery, ceramics, woodwork, leatherwork, or metalwork, made with care and ritualistic intention.

Offerings of Flowers and Natural Elements: Flowers, fresh herbs, leaves, branches, stones, crystals, shells, and other elements of nature, offered in recognition of the beauty, strength, and sacredness of the natural world.

Flowers: Seasonal, wild or cultivated, chosen for their beauty, fragrance, or symbolic association with the deity or spirit honored.

Fresh Herbs: Branches of aromatic or medicinal herbs, offered for their specific properties and energies.

Earth Elements: Stones, crystals, earth, moss, representing the connection with nature and the primordial force of the earth.

Offerings of Actions and Devotion: Offerings do not need to be only material. Acts of service, devotional practices, and expressions of virtue can also be powerful and meaningful offerings.

Time Dedicated to Spiritual Practice: Time dedicated to meditation, prayer, study of the Celtic tradition, practice of rituals, and other devotional activities.

Acts of Kindness and Compassion: Actions for the benefit of other beings, acts of charity, volunteering, community service, performed in the name of the deity or as an expression of devotion.

Development of Virtues: Conscious effort to cultivate virtues such as courage, wisdom, justice, generosity, honor, and hospitality, reflecting Celtic values and honoring divine qualities.

The way the offering is made is as important as the gift itself. The offering should be made with sincere intention, respect, and awareness. Some tips for making meaningful offerings:

Choose the Offering with Intention: Reflect on the deity or spirit you are honoring and choose an offering that is appropriate for their nature, attributes, and domains. Also consider the intention of your ritual and choose offerings that resonate with that purpose.

Prepare the Offering with Care: Dedicate time and attention to the preparation of the offering. If it is food, prepare it with care and positive intention. If it is a handcrafted object, make it with dedication and care. The energy invested in preparing the offering is also a form of devotion.

Present the Offering with Respect: When presenting the offering, do so with respect and reverence. Present it in an appropriate container, place it on the altar or in the designated place with care and attention.

Verbalize the Offering: When presenting the offering, verbalize your intention and gratitude. Say aloud or in your mind to whom you are offering, the purpose of the offering, and your gratitude for their presence and assistance.

Connect with the Energy of the Offering: After presenting the offering, take a moment to connect with its energy and visualize its acceptance by the spiritual world. Feel the exchange of energies and the reciprocity that is established.

The placement of offerings can vary depending on the type of offering and the context of the ritual. Offerings of food and drink are generally placed on the altar or in a nearby location, in clean and appropriate containers. Offerings of incense are burned in appropriate incense burners, allowing the smoke to rise and spread throughout the sacred space. Offerings of natural elements can be arranged on the altar, around the magic circle, or in specific locations in nature, depending on the ritual intention.

The disposal of offerings after the ritual is also important and should be done with respect. Food offerings that have been consecrated can be consumed by the practitioner or shared with other people or with nature, depending on the tradition and intention. Drink offerings can be poured onto the earth as a return to nature or consumed ritually. Incense offerings naturally dissipate with the smoke. Offerings of natural elements can be left at the place where they were offered, as a return to nature. Handmade offerings can be kept on the altar as devotional objects or disposed of respectfully, if necessary.

Thus, we understand that Celtic offerings, more than mere rituals of giving, are living expressions of the interaction between the material and spiritual worlds. Each gift offered carries with it the energy and intention of the giver, establishing invisible bridges of connection with the gods, the spirits of nature, and the ancestors. This ancient practice teaches us that devotion is not limited to words or prayers, but also manifests itself in concrete gestures, in the careful choice of what is given, and in the sincere willingness to share, without expecting an immediate reward, but trusting in the wisdom of cosmic reciprocity.

By bringing this tradition into the present day, we become part of an ancestral current that recognizes the value of gratitude and respect for the sacred. Each offering, whether a simple sprig of herbs or a meticulously crafted piece of art, represents not only a symbolic act, but a reaffirmation of our commitment to the harmony and balance of the universe. The way we offer, the care in the intention, and the respect for the destination of the offerings after the ritual are as essential as the elements offered themselves, as they reflect our true understanding of the sacredness of this practice.

In this way, by integrating offerings into our spiritual journey, we strengthen bonds not only with the entities we revere, but also with our own essence and with the web of existence that connects us to all that lives. Honoring this tradition is to remember that giving and receiving are part of the same cycle, where each gesture of generosity echoes in time and becomes a lasting link between the visible and the invisible.

Chapter 22
Tools of Power and Magic

On the journey through ancestral Celtic wisdom, after contemplating the essence of gifts and offerings as links to the spiritual realm, we are now led to explore an equally vital domain: the universe of ritual instruments. These objects, imbued with meaning and purpose, transcend mere functionality, revealing themselves as keys that open doors to other realities. Contrary to what a superficial observation might suggest, Celtic ritual instruments are not restricted to the role of adornments in ancient ceremonies or inert tools of a distant past. On the contrary, they manifest as dynamic catalysts, centers of personal power, and reservoirs of energy, designed to assist the practitioner in the art of concentrating their will, modulating the currents of invisible forces, and establishing direct communication with the dimensions of the sacred.

The true nature of these instruments lies in their ability to act as tangible extensions of the individual's psyche, amplifying their presence and intention in the fabric of reality. Each ritual tool, from the simplest to the most elaborate, is meticulously charged with specific symbolism and consecrated for a well-defined purpose within the magical-religious context. In this way, it becomes a portal, a channel through which the intention of the magician or devotee can flow with greater power and precision. Whether in the delimitation of a sacred space, the invocation of spiritual entities, the manipulation of subtle energy flows, or the realization of the objectives intrinsic to each ritual, these instruments act as indispensable mediators, facilitating the interaction between the tangible world and the ethereal spheres.

A deep understanding of the symbolism inherent in each instrument, the correct techniques for their use, and the consecration rites that invest them with power, are not just mere academic details for the student of the Celtic tradition. In fact, this knowledge represents the key to unlocking a deeper level of magical and devotional practice. By consciously incorporating these elements into their spiritual journey, the practitioner not only enriches their experience but also confers greater authenticity and effectiveness to their quest for the sacred. Thus, armed with this wisdom, the explorer of the Celtic path advances with greater confidence and conviction, deepening their connection with the ancestral roots of their spirituality.

Celtic ritual instruments act as extensions of the practitioner's will and intention. They are tools that amplify personal power, direct magical energy, and facilitate communication with the spiritual world. Each instrument, charged with specific symbolism and consecrated for a ritualistic purpose, becomes a channel for the manifestation of the magician's or devotee's intention, assisting in the creation of sacred space, the invocation of deities, the manipulation of energies, and the realization of the ritual's objectives.

Beyond being amplifiers of personal power, Celtic ritual instruments function as bridges between the visible and the invisible worlds. They are tangible symbols that represent abstract concepts and subtle energies of the spiritual world, helping the practitioner to connect with these dimensions in a more conscious and focused way. By using a consecrated ritual instrument, the practitioner transcends ordinary reality and enters a state of ritualistic consciousness, opening themselves to interaction with the forces and entities of the spiritual world.

Each Celtic ritual instrument has a specific symbolism and is associated with particular qualities, energies, and elements. The choice of instruments to be used in a ritual depends on the intention of the practice, the deities or spirits invoked, and the personal preference of the practitioner. Some of the most common Celtic ritual instruments and their symbolisms include:

Athame (Ritual Knife): One of the most emblematic instruments of modern Celtic magical practice, the athame is a double-edged ritual knife, usually with a black handle, used to direct energy, trace magic circles, cut energetic ties, and work with the element of Air (in some traditions) or Fire (in others). The athame symbolizes will, action, the power of decision, mental clarity, and the ability to direct magical energy. It is not used for physical cutting, being a purely symbolic and energetic tool.

Magic Wand (Staff): The wand is an instrument of personal power, used to direct energy, invoke deities, command spirits, heal, and perform other magical acts. Usually made of wood (such as willow, elder, hazel, or apple), the wand symbolizes connection with nature, growth, healing, magical authority, and the ability to channel the vital energy of the earth and spirit.

Chalice (Grail): The chalice, or grail, is a sacred container used to hold ritual liquids (water, wine, mead, etc.), representing the element of Water, the feminine principle, fertility, intuition, emotions, and the receptacle of life. The chalice symbolizes abundance, nourishment, emotional healing, introspection, and the ability to receive and contain divine energies.

Pentacle (Disc): The pentacle is a disc, usually made of wood, metal, or ceramic, adorned with a pentagram (five-pointed star). It represents the element of Earth, the material world, protection, stability, prosperity, and the physical body. The pentacle symbolizes connection with the earth, manifestation in the physical plane, security, grounding, and protection against negative energies.

Cauldron: The cauldron, as seen in the symbolism of Dagda, is a magical container associated with transformation, abundance, wisdom, rebirth, and the Otherworld. Used to prepare potions, incense, burn offerings, or as a focal point for rituals of transformation and healing. The cauldron symbolizes the womb of the Goddess, the cauldron of life and death, alchemical transformation, deep intuition, and access to ancestral knowledge.

Incense Burner: Used to burn incense and aromatic herbs, the incense burner represents the element of Air, purification, spiritual communication, elevation of consciousness, and connection with the spirit world. The smoke of incense symbolizes the ascension of prayers and intentions to the heavens, the purification of the environment, and the creation of a sacred atmosphere.

Candles: Candles represent the element of Fire, light, passion, vital energy, transformation, and the divine presence. Used to illuminate the sacred space, direct intention, represent elements or deities, and create a magical and atmospheric environment. The colors of the candles can be chosen according to the intention of the ritual and the correspondence with the desired energies.

Drum and Other Musical Instruments: The drum, bell, rattle, flute, and other musical instruments are used to create rhythm, raise energy, induce altered states of consciousness, facilitate meditation, invoke spirits, and celebrate joy and dance in the ritual. Music and sound are powerful tools to connect the practitioner with the energetic flow of the universe and with the vibration of the sacred.

Choosing your own ritual instruments is a personal and intuitive process. There is no "recipe" for choosing the perfect instruments, but some tips can help in this process:

Connect with the Symbolism: Study the symbolism of each instrument and reflect on how it resonates with your own practice and ritual intentions.

Choose instruments that attract you intuitively and that connect with your personal understanding of Celtic magic and spirituality.

Quality and Material: Prefer instruments made of natural materials, such as wood, metal, stone, ceramic, or glass, which vibrate with more subtle and authentic energies. Look for good quality instruments that are durable and that inspire confidence and respect.

Intuition and Attraction: Trust your intuition when choosing your instruments. Visit esoteric shops, craft fairs, or even nature, and observe which objects attract you, call your attention, and awaken a special feeling in you. The "right" instrument usually manifests itself through an internal resonance, an intuitive recognition of your connection with the tool.

Handmade or Acquired: Handmade instruments, created by the practitioner themselves, carry a personal energy and a deeper connection with the ritualistic intention. However, instruments purchased in specialized stores can also be consecrated and personalized to become tools of personal power.

Consecrating ritual instruments is an essential step to transform them from ordinary objects into magical and sacred tools. Consecration is a ritual of dedication and blessing, which infuses the instrument with spiritual energy, connects it with the ritualistic purpose, and makes it a channel for the manifestation of the practitioner's intention. Consecration generally involves the following steps:

Cleaning and Purification: Physically clean the instrument and purify it energetically, using the purification techniques we have already explored (fire, water, air, and earth).

Elemental Consecration: Consecrate the instrument to the four elements, invoking the energies of each element and asking them to bless and empower the tool. The instrument can be passed through the smoke of incense (Air), sprinkled with water (Water), quickly passed through the flame of a candle (Fire), and touched to the earth or salt (Earth).

Consecration to the Deity (Optional): Dedicate the instrument to a specific Celtic deity, invoking their presence and asking for their blessing and protection for the tool.

Naming (Optional): Give the instrument a name, creating a personal and intimate connection with the magic tool.

Charging with Intention: Visualize personal energy and ritualistic intention flowing into the instrument, charging it with the desired magical power.

Respectful Storage: Store the ritual instruments in a clean, safe, and respectful place, such as an altar, a special box, or a sacred cloth, protecting them from profane energies and maintaining their energetic integrity.

By understanding the depth and purpose of Celtic ritual instruments, we realize that they are not just tools, but extensions of the practitioner's own essence. Each object, chosen or created with intention, becomes a link between the visible and the invisible, allowing energy to flow in a more harmonious and directed way. Ritual practice, when enriched by these consecrated instruments, strengthens the connection with deities, spirits, and elements, creating a sacred space where magic and devotion manifest with greater clarity and intensity.

More than the possession of these objects, the true power lies in the bond established with them and the intention that animates them. An athame is not just a blade, but the materialization of will; a chalice is not just a container, but a portal to the abundance of the spirit. In this way, the Celtic practitioner learns that every ritualistic gesture, every touch on a sacred instrument, reverberates in the web of existence, expanding their influence over the forces that govern reality. Thus, the practice becomes not just a symbolic ceremony, but a profound dialogue between the human and the divine.

By integrating these instruments into their spiritual path, the devotee strengthens their own presence in the magical world and in the ancestral tradition that guides them. More than mere artifacts, they are witnesses and conductors of the sacred journey, reminding us that the true power is not in the objects themselves, but in the connection and intention that make them alive. With this understanding, the practitioner moves forward, aware that their quest for the sacred is woven both in the visible acts and in the invisible energy that moves them.

Chapter 23
Introspection and Spiritual Connection

In initiatory journeys, after the conscious manipulation of the tangible world through rituals and external symbols, the adept is invited to turn inward, to explore the inner landscapes of the mind and spirit. If ritual instruments represent the alchemy of the concrete plane, meditative and visualization practices constitute mastery over the subjective realm, the dominion of the subtle energies that shape reality. This is the threshold of a new cycle in the spiritual quest, a transition from the manifest to the latent, from the visible to the invisible, where true power resides not in objects or spoken words, but in the innate ability to connect with the deep currents of consciousness.

Within the ancient Celtic tradition, meditation and visualization transcend the mere search for tranquility or mental focus; they are arcane portals that lead to the essence of the Self and the interconnected web of existence. These practices represent the art of quieting the inner turmoil to listen to the silent voice of intuition, of refining perception beyond the ordinary senses, and of forging an intimate connection with the primordial forces that animate nature and the cosmos. They are not passive relaxation techniques, but dynamic methods of exploring consciousness, of dialoguing with the spiritual world, and of expanding the limits of one's own identity.

Thus, immersing oneself in the study and practice of Celtic meditation and visualization is to tread a path of profound transformation. It is to open the doors to a broader understanding of reality, to unveil the ancestral wisdom dormant in the depths of the spirit, and to experience, directly and unequivocally, the sacred dimension that permeates all things. By cultivating these internal tools, the seeker not only enriches their personal journey but also empowers themselves to manifest their highest potential, aligned with the flow of life and in harmony with cosmic energies.

Meditation, in the Celtic context, takes various forms, but in its essence, it aims to quiet the mind, calm the constant flow of thoughts and emotions, and direct the focus of consciousness to the present moment, to the breath, to a sound, an image, or to the vastness of the Self. Celtic meditation is not necessarily sitting still in silence, but can include active practices, such as meditative walks in nature, ritual dances, or manual work performed with mindfulness. The main objective is to cultivate a state of conscious presence, receptivity, and connection with the flow of life and the energy of the spirit.

The purposes and benefits of Celtic meditation are vast and comprehensive:

Introspection and Self-Knowledge: Meditation offers an internal space of silence and clarity, allowing the practitioner to observe their own thoughts, emotions, behavioral patterns, and limiting beliefs with greater objectivity and discernment. Through meditative introspection, it is possible to deepen self-knowledge, identify areas of personal growth, and awaken to one's own divine essence.

Spiritual Connection: Meditation facilitates direct connection with the Celtic spiritual world, with the gods and goddesses, nature spirits, and revered ancestors. In deep meditative states, the veil between the worlds becomes thinner, allowing for intuitive communication, the reception of spiritual messages and guidance, and the experience of the divine presence.

Emotional and Mental Balance: The regular practice of Celtic meditation assists in the management of stress, anxiety, mental agitation, and emotional instability. By calming the mind and body, meditation promotes inner balance, inner peace, serenity, and emotional resilience.

Expansion of Consciousness: Celtic meditation can expand consciousness beyond the limits of the rational mind and ego, opening perception to other dimensions of reality, to the interconnectedness of all things, and to the vastness of the inner and outer universe. The expansion of meditative consciousness can lead to profound insights, intuitive understanding, and the experience of unity with the All.

Development of Intuition: By quieting the logical and rational mind, Celtic meditation allows intuition, the inner voice of wisdom, to manifest with greater clarity and sharpness. Regular meditative practice strengthens intuitive ability, enhancing decision-making, problem-solving, and guidance on the journey of life.

Grounding and Centering: Some Celtic meditation techniques, especially those based on nature, aid in energetic grounding, connection with the energy of the earth, and centering in the present moment. Meditative grounding and centering promote emotional stability, a sense of security, and conscious presence in the physical body and the material world.

Celtic meditation techniques are diverse and can be adapted to the preferences and needs of each practitioner. Some types of Celtic meditation and visualization include:

Nature Meditation: Practiced in sacred natural places, such as forests, rivers, lakes, beaches, or open fields. The practitioner sits, walks, or simply remains in silence in nature, focusing on the breath, the sounds of the environment, the sensations of the body, and the beauty of the landscape. Nature meditation connects the practitioner with the energies of the earth, sky, water, and air, promoting grounding, centering, and harmonization with natural rhythms.

Meditation with the Elements: Concentration on one of the four elements (Earth, Air, Fire, and Water), visualizing their energy, breathing their essence, and attuning to their qualities. For example, meditating with the Earth element might involve visualizing roots growing from the base of the spine towards the center of the earth, feeling stability and security. Meditating with the Water element might involve visualizing oneself bathing in a crystal-clear river, feeling purification and emotional fluidity.

Guided Meditation with Celtic Deities: Use of guided visualizations that lead the practitioner to meet a specific Celtic deity in an imaginary sacred place, seeking their guidance, blessing, or healing. For example, a guided meditation with Brigid might lead the practitioner to a sacred garden where the goddess welcomes them, offers water from a healing spring, and inspires their creativity.

Meditation with Celtic Sounds and Chants: Use of music, chants, mantras, or sounds of nature (such as the sound of waterfalls, the wind in the trees, or the singing of birds) to induce meditative states and facilitate connection with the spiritual world. Sound and music can vibrate the body, calm the mind, and open the heart to the experience of the sacred. The Celtic shamanic drum, in particular, is frequently used to induce altered states of consciousness and facilitate meditative journeys.

Creative Visualization and Shamanic Journeys: Use of guided imagery to create internal scenarios, meet with spirit guides, travel to other worlds (such as the Celtic Otherworld or elemental realms), and explore inner landscapes in search of wisdom, healing, or transformation. Celtic shamanic journeys can be undertaken with the aid of the drum, chants, or other musical instruments, and may involve encounters with power animals, nature spirits, or ancestral deities.

Practical tips for starting the practice of Celtic meditation and visualization:

Start Small and Be Regular: Begin with short sessions of 5 to 10 minutes and gradually increase the time as you feel more comfortable. Regularity is more important than the initial duration. Try to meditate daily, even if for a few minutes, to cultivate the habit and reap the benefits of consistent practice.

Choose a Quiet and Comfortable Place: Find a place where you can meditate without interruptions, where you feel safe and relaxed. It can be an indoor space dedicated to your Celtic altar, a quiet corner of your home, or a natural place outdoors.

Comfortable Posture: Sit in a comfortable posture, with your spine erect but relaxed. You can sit in a chair, on a cushion on the floor, or on a meditation bench. If the seated posture is uncomfortable, you can meditate lying down or walking slowly.

Focus on the Breath: The breath is an anchor for the mind in the present moment. Concentrate on the sensation of the breath entering and leaving the body, observing the natural and gentle rhythm of your breathing. When the mind wanders, gently redirect the focus back to the breath.

Be Gentle with Yourself: The mind will wander during meditation, and that is perfectly normal. Do not criticize or frustrate yourself when thoughts arise. Just observe them gently and gently redirect the focus back to your anchor (breath, sound, image, etc.). Meditation is a practice of patience, persistence, and self-compassion.

Experiment with Different Techniques: Explore different types of Celtic meditation and visualization to discover which ones resonate best with you and your needs. Vary your practices, try new techniques, and find your own meditative path.

Meditation and Celtic visualization are powerful tools for the spiritual journey, offering paths to introspection, self-knowledge, connection with the sacred, and expansion of consciousness. By integrating these practices into their daily routine and Celtic rituals, the modern disciple deepens their spiritual experience, strengthens their connection with the invisible world, and treads the path of devotion with clarity, presence, and inner wisdom.

As the practitioner delves deeper into Celtic meditation and visualization, they discover that these practices are not just mental exercises, but living experiences of communion with the sacred. Each inner journey reveals hidden layers of their own essence, bringing to light perceptions previously veiled by the rush of everyday life. Silence becomes a space of revelation, where the spirit can dialogue with the gods, ancestors, and primordial forces of nature. It is in this conscious stillness that ancient wisdom resurfaces, guiding the seeker on their journey of growth and transformation.

Consistent practice strengthens intuition, expands perception, and allows the individual to align with the rhythms of the universe. Gradually, they realize that they are not isolated, but interwoven with the great web of existence, where everything is connected. The messages received in visions, the insights that emerge from silence, and the spiritual encounters experienced during meditations become part of their reality, shaping their way of interacting with the visible and invisible world. Celtic spirituality, then, ceases to be a distant knowledge and becomes an experience deeply rooted in being.

Thus, those who tread this path realize that meditation and visualization are not just ritual practices, but portals to a deeper understanding of life. By cultivating introspection and spiritual connection, they become a link between past and present, between earth and sky, between human and divine. The inner journey, always in motion, invites them to continue exploring, discovering, and awakening to the eternal wisdom that echoes in the mists of time.

Chapter 24
The Continuing Journey

In an invisible fabric that connects the pulse of the cosmos with the simplicity of the instant, we find an ancestral invitation, a call that echoes through time and directs us beyond the boundaries of the known. Unveiling the fullness of existence does not reside solely in moments of solemn introspection or in the search for transcendental revelations in isolated spaces. The vital essence of the journey manifests itself in the mundanity of breathing, in the rhythm of heartbeats, in the intricate web of human interactions, and in the constant dance with the world around us. It is on this vast and mysterious everyday stage that the genuine adventure reveals itself: learning to choreograph the immemorial principles in every gesture, in every reflection, in every connection with others and with the web of life.

This is the threshold of a profound exploration, a dive into the subtle currents that irrigate existence and invite us to awaken to the hidden symphony that pulses in every atom of the universe. It is not about deciphering formulas or embracing rigid dogmas, but rather about internalizing a philosophy of life that reverberates with timeless values. Harmony with nature, reverence for the ancestors who preceded us, the search for an intimate dialogue with the primordial forces, the art of weaving magic into the ordinary, and the incessant pursuit of balance and consonance. These are the pillars that support the architecture of this path, a compassionate guide for those who yearn to incorporate these principles into every action, every choice, every posture before the tapestry of life.

Integrating this ancient wisdom into the frenetic rhythm of the now is an alchemical process, a continuous dance of learning, adaptation, and inner blossoming. Celtic ancestry, more than a reliquary of archaic rites, reveals itself as a star map for the individual and collective journey. It is a compass that points to the rediscovery of the sacredness inherent in existence, an invitation to experience each dawn and each dusk with the reverence that life itself evokes. In this immersion, we will unveil the practical ways to intertwine magic and devotion in every fragment of everyday life, transforming the commonplace into a portal to the extraordinary.

Celtic spirituality, as we have seen, is not a set of rigid dogmas or inflexible rules, but rather a philosophy of life based on fundamental values such as connection with nature, honor to ancestors, devotion to deities, the practice of magic, and the search for balance and harmony. Integrating Celtic spirituality into daily life means incorporating these values into our daily actions, our choices, and our way of being in the world. It is a continuous process of learning, adaptation, and personal growth, where ancient Celtic wisdom becomes a guide for our individual and collective journey.

There are several practical ways to integrate Celtic spirituality into everyday life, weaving magic and devotion into every aspect of our lives:

Connecting with Nature Daily:

The connection with nature is the heart of Celtic spirituality. Integrating this connection into daily life does not necessarily mean living in a forest or climbing mountains every day, but rather cultivating awareness of nature in our surroundings, in whatever environment we find ourselves.

Time Outdoors: Dedicate time daily to being in contact with nature, even if it's just for a few minutes. Walk in a park, sit in a garden, observe the trees, plants, birds, sky, and water. Allow yourself to feel the energy of nature, breathe the fresh air, and reconnect with the natural rhythm of the world.

Conscious Observation: Develop the habit of observing nature around you with full attention. Notice the details of the leaves, the colors of the flowers, the movement of the wind, the sound of the birds. Perceive the beauty and sacredness that manifest in every detail of the natural world, even in urban environments.

Bring Nature Inside: Incorporate natural elements into your home and work environment. Have plants, flowers, stones, crystals, wood, and moving water (fountains, aquariums). Create a small natural altar in your house, with objects that represent nature and its energies.

Respect and Gratitude: Cultivate respect and gratitude for nature in all its forms. Recognize the interdependence between humans and the environment, practice sustainability, reduce your environmental impact, and give thanks daily for the gifts of nature that sustain your life.

Honoring the Natural Cycles and Celtic Festivals:

Celtic spirituality is intrinsically linked to the cycles of nature and the rhythms of the seasons. Integrating this connection into everyday life means being attentive to natural cycles and celebrating the Celtic festivals of the Wheel of the Year, honoring the energies of each season and the ancestral wisdom they carry.

Follow the Cycles of the Moon and Sun: Observe the phases of the moon, the changing of the seasons, the equinoxes and solstices. Tune into the lunar and solar rhythm, noticing how they influence your energy, your mood, and your personal cycle.

Celebrate the Festivals of the Celtic Wheel of the Year: Mark the festivals of Samhain, Yule, Imbolc, Ostara, Beltane, Litha, Lughnasadh, and Mabon on your calendar. Research the meanings and traditional rituals of each festival and adapt the celebrations to your own practice and context. Celebrate with simple rituals at home, with friends, or in local Celtic communities.

Personal Seasonal Rituals: Create personal rituals to mark the changing of the seasons, honor the energy of the present moment, and set intentions for the cycle that is beginning. Perform rituals outdoors, connecting with nature and celebrating the beauty and wisdom of each season.

Connect with the Energies of Each Season: Explore the energies and qualities associated with each season of the year. In spring, celebrate rebirth, renewal, and new beginnings. In summer, celebrate abundance, vitality, and solar energy. In autumn, celebrate the harvest, gratitude, and introspection. In winter, celebrate gathering, rest, and preparation for the new cycle.

Cultivating Devotion and Connection with Celtic Deities:

Devotion to Celtic deities can be integrated into daily life through simple and constant practices, cultivating a personal and intimate relationship with the gods and goddesses that resonate with your soul.

Personal Altar: Create a personal altar dedicated to the Celtic deities in your home. Decorate the altar with images, symbols, and objects that represent the deities you honor. Keep candles, incense, offerings, and other devotional objects on the altar.

Daily Prayers and Invocations: Set aside a few minutes daily to connect with the deities through prayers, invocations, chants, or meditations. Ask for guidance, protection, blessings, and assistance in your daily activities. Express gratitude for the gifts received.

Study of Myths and Symbols: Deepen your knowledge of the myths, attributes, symbols, and stories of the Celtic deities. Read books, articles, participate in study groups, and connect with Celtic communities online and in person to learn and share knowledge.

Intuition and Synchronicity: Be attentive to signs, synchronicities, and messages that may arise in your day-to-day life, interpreting them as possible communications from the deities or the spiritual world. Trust your intuition and follow the insights that arise on your journey.

Practicing Everyday Magic:

Magic in Celtic spirituality is not limited to formal rituals but can be integrated into daily life as a form of conscious intention, connection with energy, and manifestation of desires in harmony with the universe.

Conscious Intention in Actions: Carry out your daily activities with conscious intention, directing your energy and focus toward the desired purpose. When cooking, visualize nutrition and well-being being infused into the food. When walking, feel the connection with the earth and the revitalizing energy of nature. When working, focus on clarity, productivity, and success.

Use Symbols and Affirmations: Incorporate Celtic symbols into your daily life, such as the Triskele, the Pentagram, the Celtic Cross, or other symbols that resonate with you. Use positive affirmations and declarations of intention to strengthen your connection with magical energy and manifest your desires.

Magic with the Elements: Use the natural elements in your daily magical practices. Light candles to direct the energy of fire, use incense to purify the environment with air, use holy water to cleanse and bless, and connect with the earth to ground and manifest intentions.

Quick and Simple Rituals: Perform quick and simple rituals at opportune moments of the day, such as protection rituals when leaving home, gratitude rituals upon receiving a blessing, healing rituals when feeling unwell, or rituals of connection with nature when contemplating the beauty of the world.

Living Celtic Values in Ethics and Relationships:

Celtic spirituality is permeated by ethical values that can guide our actions and relationships in everyday life, cultivating a more meaningful, authentic, and harmonious life.

Honor and Integrity: Seek to live with honor and integrity in all your actions, words, and relationships. Be true to your word, keep your commitments, act with honesty and ethics in all situations.

Courage and Resilience: Cultivate the courage to face life's challenges with determination and resilience. Seek the inner strength to overcome obstacles, learn from difficulties, and move forward with confidence and hope.

Wisdom and Discernment: Seek wisdom in all your experiences, learn from mistakes and successes, cultivate discernment to make wise and just decisions. Connect with the ancestral wisdom of the Celtic tradition and with your own intuition.

Hospitality and Community: Practice hospitality, welcoming and receiving others with generosity and kindness. Value community, strengthen family and social ties, and participate in Celtic groups to share knowledge and experiences.

Justice and Balance: Seek justice in your actions and relationships, treat others with equality and respect, and defend the rights of the most vulnerable. Seek balance in all areas of your life, harmonizing the needs of the body, mind, and spirit, and seeking balance between giving and receiving. Celtic spirituality, when consciously lived in everyday life, transforms into a continuous journey of learning and connection. It is not just about recreating ancient rituals or following pre-defined practices, but about finding genuine ways to intertwine this ancestral wisdom with modern life. Each intentional gesture, each thought aimed at balance, each moment of gratitude to nature and ancestors strengthens this sacred bond. Thus, spirituality ceases to be something separate from routine and becomes the invisible thread that permeates all actions, making the ordinary something deeply meaningful.

Over time, this integration is reflected in the way we deal with challenges, relate to others, and cultivate our presence in the world. Harmony with the cycles of nature teaches us patience and resilience; reverence for ancestors reminds us of the importance of roots and the legacy we leave behind; the practice of everyday magic empowers us to see beyond the surface and shape reality with awareness. In this way, Celtic spirituality becomes more than a study or a belief — it becomes a way of life, a path that guides each step with wisdom, courage, and devotion.

As we walk this path, we realize that there is no final destination, for the spiritual journey is cyclical and always transforming, just like the seasons that mark the Wheel of the Year. Each day is an opportunity to deepen our connection, to learn from the signs the universe offers us, and to express our spirituality through the choices we make. The Celtic path invites us to walk with awareness, respect, and joy, finding in the present the bridge between the past and the future, between the visible and the invisible, between the sacred and the mundane.

Chapter 25
Conduct and Responsibility

It is in the essence of the ancestral journey, pulsing in the depths of the human soul, that we find the guiding thread to walk the path of existence with purpose and meaning. An internal compass, forged in the deep roots of Celtic wisdom, emerges as a beacon to illuminate the choices and decisions that shape our earthly experience. It is not a set of inflexible dogmas, but rather a living wisdom, woven by millennial experience, that invites us to a constant dance between intimate reflection and action in the world. It is in this rhythm that the secret lies to manifesting our true nature, aligned with the rhythms of life and the symphony of the universe.

This guiding principle, essential for the contemporary disciple seeking to deepen their understanding of Celtic spirituality, manifests as an invitation to self-observation and conscious consideration of each step. Understanding the intricate web of responsibilities that connects us to the world around us, to the other consciousnesses that share this plane, and to the subtle forces that permeate reality, becomes a daily and continuous exercise. It is through this ethical lens, shaped by ancestral values and adapted to the context of the present, that we can discern the path of integrity, honoring the sacredness of life in all its manifestations. In this journey, the internal compass does not dictate laws, but rather inspires an attitude of respect, reverence, and responsibility towards the whole.

Thus, Celtic Ethics emerges, not as a static moral code, but as a dynamic and vibrant guide, which impels us to question, reflect, and act with intention and awareness. This ethical path is not imposed as a straitjacket, but rather as a living map, which unfolds with each step, revealing the beauty and complexity of the choices that shape our journey. By embracing Celtic Ethics, we invite ourselves to a deep and meaningful relationship with the world, with our fellow human beings, and with the sacred that resides in every atom of existence, cultivating integrity as a fundamental pillar of our expression in the universe.

The ethics of the modern Celtic disciple is based on ancestral values, adapted to the contemporary context and the individual journey of each practitioner. It is not about following an external and imposed moral code, but rather about cultivating an internal compass, guided by Celtic wisdom, intuition, and awareness of our responsibilities as spiritual beings and as members of the web of life. Celtic ethics is a path of self-awareness, integrity, and responsibility, which invites us to live in harmony with the values we profess and to manifest our spirituality in concrete actions in the world.

Some of the fundamental principles and values of the modern Celtic disciple's ethics include:

Honor and Integrity (Onóir agus Ionracas):

Honor and integrity are central pillars of Celtic ethics. Honoring oneself, others, one's word, ancestors, and deities is a fundamental principle that permeates all areas of the disciple's life. Integrity is manifested in the coherence between professed values and practiced actions, in honesty with oneself and others, and in the pursuit of truth and authenticity in all situations.

Honoring One's Word: Fulfilling commitments, promises, and agreements made, whether in the personal, professional, or spiritual sphere. The word of a Celtic disciple should be trustworthy and honored.

Acting with Honesty and Truth: Seeking truth in all situations, acting honestly with oneself and others, avoiding falsehood, manipulation, and dishonesty.

Respecting Oneself and Others: Valuing one's own dignity and that of others, treating oneself and others with respect, consideration, and empathy, recognizing the inherent sacredness of each being.

Honoring Ancestors and Lineage: Respecting and honoring ancestors, family and spiritual lineage, traditions, and ancestral wisdom that have been passed down to us.

Respect and Reverence for Nature (Meas agus Urraim don Dúlra):

As we have extensively explored, nature is sacred in Celtic spirituality. Respect and reverence for nature are ethical imperatives for the modern Celtic disciple, reflecting the understanding of the interconnectedness of all life and human responsibility as guardians of the planet.

Living in Harmony with Nature: Seeking to live in balance with the environment, reducing ecological impact, practicing sustainability, and adopting a lifestyle that respects natural cycles and wildlife.

Honoring the Spirits of Nature: Recognizing and respecting the presence of nature spirits in natural places, giving thanks for the gifts of the earth, and acting with consideration and care when interacting with the natural world.

Protecting and Preserving the Environment: Engaging in actions to protect and preserve the environment, supporting environmental causes, promoting ecological awareness, and defending the sacredness of nature in all its forms.

Learning from the Wisdom of Nature: Observing nature with attention, seeking wisdom in natural rhythms and cycles, learning from animals, plants, and the elements, and recognizing nature as a great spiritual teacher.

Courage and Inner Strength (Misneach agus Neart Istigh):

Courage and inner strength are valued Celtic virtues, essential for facing life's challenges, overcoming fears, and following one's own spiritual path with authenticity and determination. Celtic ethics does not preach passivity or submission, but rather the cultivation of inner strength to act with bravery and integrity in the face of adversity.

Facing Fears and Challenges: Developing the courage to face internal fears and external challenges, overcome obstacles, and move forward with confidence and resilience.

Defending What is Just and Right: Have the courage to uphold ethical principles, fight for justice, protect the most vulnerable, and take a position against injustice and oppression.

Following One's Own Spiritual Path: Having the courage to follow one's own spiritual path with authenticity, even if it is different from the path of the majority, trusting one's own intuition and the guidance of the heart.

Living with Authenticity and Truth: Being true to oneself, living according to one's own values and principles, expressing one's own truth and authenticity in the world, without being overly influenced by the opinions of others.

Wisdom and the Pursuit of Knowledge (Eagna agus Lorg na hEolais):

Wisdom and the pursuit of knowledge are important intellectual and spiritual values in Celtic ethics. The Celtic disciple is encouraged to seek knowledge from various sources, to develop discernment, to cultivate an open mind, and to seek ancestral wisdom to guide their journey.

Seeking Knowledge and Wisdom: Dedicating oneself to the study of Celtic tradition, myths, ritual practices, history, and Celtic philosophy. Seeking knowledge from various sources, including books, oral teachings, personal experiences, and the wisdom of nature.

Developing Discernment: Cultivating the ability to discern truth from falsehood, good from evil, the essential from the superficial. Developing critical thinking, the ability to analyze, and intuition to make wise and just decisions.

Open Mind and Curiosity: Keeping an open mind to new ideas, perspectives, and experiences. Cultivating curiosity, questioning, and the search for answers to the big questions of life.

Sharing Knowledge Responsibly: Sharing acquired knowledge and wisdom with others, in an ethical and responsible manner, respecting the individuality and path of each person.

Hospitality and Community (Fáilte agus Pobal):

Hospitality and community are essential social values in Celtic ethics. Welcoming others with generosity, practicing hospitality, strengthening community ties, and valuing the interconnection between human beings are principles that promote social harmony and collective well-being.

Practicing Hospitality: Welcoming others with generosity, offering help and support to those in need, sharing resources and goods with those who need them. Celtic hospitality extends to all, including strangers, travelers and those seeking refuge.

Strengthening Community Ties: Valuing the community, participating in Celtic groups, collaborating on community projects, strengthening family and social ties, and seeking harmony and cooperation between individuals and groups.

Promoting Social Justice and Equality: Defending social justice, equality, inclusion and respect for diversity. Fight against discrimination, oppression and injustice in all its forms.

Cultivating Compassion and Empathy: Developing the ability to put yourself in another person's shoes, understand their pains and joys, practice compassion and empathy in all relationships.

Balance and Moderation (Cothromaíocht agus Measarthacht):

Balance and moderation are principles that govern Celtic ethics, seeking harmony in all areas of life, avoiding excesses, imbalances, and extremes. The Celtic disciple seeks balance between the material and spiritual worlds, between action and contemplation, between giving and receiving, and between the various facets of their own nature.

Seeking Balance in All Areas of Life: Harmonizing the needs of the body, mind, and spirit, balancing work and rest, action and contemplation, social life and time for solitude, seeking a full and integrated life.

Avoiding Excesses and Imbalances: Practicing moderation in all aspects of life, avoiding excesses, vices, greed, selfishness, and other forms of imbalance that harm oneself and others.

Cultivating Patience and Serenity: Developing patience, serenity, and the ability to deal with life's challenges and unforeseen events with calm and emotional balance.

Living in the Present with Awareness: Practicing mindfulness, living the present moment with awareness, savoring the joys of life, and dealing with challenges with presence and discernment.

The ethics of the modern Celtic disciple is a work in progress, a personal and collective journey of learning, reflection, and continuous improvement. There are no ready-made answers or magic formulas, and each disciple is invited to interpret and apply these ethical principles to their own life, seeking inner wisdom, the guidance of the Celtic tradition, and the inspiration of their own heart. Celtic ethics is not a heavy burden, but rather a luminous guide, that leads us to a fuller, more meaningful, and harmonious life, in connection with the sacred, with nature, with others, and with ourselves.

By treading the path of conduct and responsibility within Celtic spirituality, we understand that every action resonates in the invisible web of existence. It is not just about following principles inherited from the ancients, but about living them authentically in the present, adapting them to the needs and challenges of the contemporary world. Celtic ethics teaches us that true honor lies not only in words, but in the coherence between thought, intention, and attitude. Thus, we cultivate not only respect for others and for nature, but also a deep commitment to our own growth and integrity.

This journey, however, is neither linear nor free of challenges. The balance between courage and compassion, justice and flexibility, tradition and renewal requires constant reflection and self-knowledge. Celtic ethics is not imposed as a weight, but as a compass, guiding us through uncertainties, reminding us that each choice shapes not only our individual destiny, but the flow of energy around us. Assuming this responsibility means recognizing our role in the great dance of life, where every gesture of respect, generosity, and truth becomes a sacred act.

Thus, by integrating these values into daily life, we realize that Celtic spirituality is not limited to rites or the words written in ancient myths. It manifests itself in the way we walk through the world, in the way we treat those who cross our path, and in the reverence we nurture for life in all its forms. Ethical conduct, then, ceases to be an abstract concept and becomes a living reflection of the connection between the human and the divine, leading us to a fuller, more meaningful existence aligned with the eternal cycles of nature and the spirit.

Chapter 26
Next Steps on the Celtic Journey

Here a cycle ends, but not a journey. The ancestral teachings you have absorbed so far are not an end point, but rather the prelude to a deeper, more personal exploration. Imagine that you are on the verge of a portal, a threshold that separates acquired knowledge from lived wisdom. This portal, adorned with the symbols and mysteries of the Celtic tradition, invites you to transcend theory and embrace practice, to transform information into sacred experience. Prepare, therefore, to take the next steps, no longer as a curious explorer, but as a pilgrim in search of enlightenment.

Now, the path ahead reveals itself less like a detailed map and more like a flowing river, with its unexpected curves, challenging rapids, and pools of serene contemplation. The Celtic journey, in its essence, is not about following predefined trails, but about learning to navigate the waters of intuition, guided by the inner compass of your spirit. Do not expect rigid instructions or magic formulas; instead, sharpen your senses, trust your perception, and allow the ancestral wisdom to resonate at your own pace, in your own voice. From this point on, personalization becomes the key, adaptation the art, and direct experience your greatest teacher.

Be aware that spiritual growth is not a straight upward line, but an ever-expanding spiral. There will be moments of radiant clarity and inspiration, as well as moments of doubt and inner darkness. Both are equally valuable, as each cycle of light and shadow contributes to the unique tapestry of your journey. Embrace the totality of the experience, the joys and the challenges, the certainties and the uncertainties. Allow Celtic wisdom to be not only a body of knowledge, but a lens through which you interpret life itself, an ethical code that shapes your actions, and a perennial source of strength and inspiration at every step of the way.

From this point on, your Celtic journey becomes increasingly personal and intuitive. There is no "right way" or a single formula to follow, and each disciple is invited to explore, experiment and adapt the Celtic practices and teachings to their own individuality, their needs and their unique connection with the sacred.

To continue your journey in Celtic Spirituality, consider the following next steps and resources:

Deepening Knowledge: Continuous study is essential to deepen your understanding of Celtic Spirituality and enrich your practice. Explore the following resources to expand your knowledge:

Books and Texts: Immerse yourself in reading books on Celtic mythology, history, rituals, magical practices, philosophy, and spirituality. Explore both academic works and practical books and study guides. Some suggestions of authors and themes:

Celtic Mythology: "Celtic Mythology" by Miranda Green, "The Mabinogion," "Táin Bó Cúailnge" (The Cattle Raid of Cooley).

Modern Spirituality and Druidry: "The Path of Druidry" by Emma Restall Orr, "A Druid's Path" by Philip Carr-Gomm, "Pagan Portals - Celtic Witchcraft: Modern Witchcraft Meets Celtic Ways" by Mabh Savage.

Celtic Shamanism: "Celtic Shamanism" by D.J. Conway, "Plant Spirit Shamanism: Traditional Techniques for Healing the Soul" by Ross Heaven.

Celtic Herbalism and Medicine: "Celtic Tree Magic" by Danu Forest, "The Celtic Herbal" by Margaret Elphinstone.

Celtic Folklore and Traditions: "The Lore of the Land: A Guide to England's Legends, from Springhead to Windgather" by Jennifer Westwood and Jacqueline Simpson, "Irish Folktales" by Jeremiah Curtin.

Courses and Workshops: Participate in courses, workshops, and lectures on topics related to Celtic spirituality, taught by authors, experienced practitioners, and Celtic communities. Look for online or in-person events in your area or in online Celtic communities.

Websites and Blogs: Explore websites, blogs, and online portals dedicated to Celtic spirituality, which offer articles, essays, information, resources, and virtual communities of practitioners.

Study and Reading Groups: Form or participate in study and reading groups on Celtic themes with other interested people. Share knowledge, discuss books and texts, exchange ideas, and deepen your understanding together.

Deepening Ritual Practice: Ritual practice is the beating heart of Celtic spirituality. Continue to develop and improve your ritual practice through the following suggestions:

Regular Rituals: Establish a regular ritual practice, even if it is simple and short, whether daily, weekly, or seasonal. Perform rituals of devotion, meditation, connection with nature, celebration of Celtic festivals, or for specific purposes.

Experiment with Different Rituals and Formats:

Explore different types of Celtic rituals, experiment with various formats, adapt the structures and ritual elements to your own intuition and creativity. Don't be afraid to innovate and personalize your practice.

Deepen the Connection with the Deities:

Dedicate time to connect with the Celtic deities that you feel most drawn to. Perform specific rituals in honor of each deity, study their myths and attributes, meditate on their energy, and seek their guidance.

Develop your Ritual Language: Improve your invocations, prayers, chants, and visualizations. Create your own words of power, rhymes, poems, and devotional songs. Allow your creativity to flow and enrich your ritual expression.

Work with Consecrated Ritual Tools: Continue to use and improve the use of your ritual tools. Consecrate new instruments that resonate with you, explore different techniques of energy manipulation, and deepen your connection with the magical power of ritual tools.

Practice Meditation and Visualization Regularly:

Incorporate Celtic meditation and visualization into your daily routine as a fundamental practice of introspection, spiritual connection, and development of consciousness. Experiment with different techniques and find those that best suit you.

Connecting with the Celtic Community: Celtic spirituality is also experienced in community, through the exchange of knowledge, the sharing of experiences, and mutual support among practitioners. Explore the following ways to connect with the Celtic community:

Local Celtic Groups and Circles: Look for Celtic groups, circles, or groves in your area. Participate in meetings, community rituals, festival celebrations, and cultural events. Connect with other practitioners, share experiences, and strengthen your journey together.

Online Communities: Participate in online Celtic communities, forums, discussion groups, social networks, and virtual platforms dedicated to Celtic spirituality. Interact with practitioners from all over the world, exchange ideas, ask questions, share knowledge, and find support and inspiration.

Celtic Festivals and Gatherings: Participate in larger, regional, national, or international Celtic festivals, gatherings, and events. Have the opportunity to meet practitioners from various traditions, participate in workshops, rituals, and large-scale celebrations, and experience the energy of the Celtic community in its entirety.

Mentors and Teachers: Seek mentors, teachers, or experienced practitioners who can guide and advise you on your Celtic journey. Look for people who inspire trust, respect, and wisdom, and who can offer you teachings, advice, and individualized support.

Exploring Specific Traditions and Paths: Within the vast landscape of Celtic spirituality, there are several specific traditions, lineages, and paths that you can explore and deepen, according to your interests and affinities:

Druidry: Explore the different modern Druidic orders and traditions, such as the Ancient Order of Druids in America (AODA), the Order of Bards, Ovates and Druids (OBOD), or Ár nDraíocht Féine (ADF). Investigate the teachings, practices, and structures of each order and find out if any of them resonate with you.

Celtic Wicca: If you are drawn to Wicca and witchcraft practices, explore Celtic Wicca, which integrates elements of the Celtic tradition with the principles and practices of modern Wicca. Research the different lineages and traditions of Celtic Wicca and find out if this path calls to you.

Celtic Reconstructionism: If you have an academic and historical inclination, explore Celtic Reconstructionism, which seeks to reconstruct the practices and beliefs of the ancient Celtic religion based on historical, archaeological, and folkloric sources. Delve into the study of ancient Celtic languages, original texts, and archaeological evidence.

Celtic Shamanism: If you are drawn to shamanic practices and connection with the spirit world through altered states of consciousness, explore Celtic Shamanism, which integrates shamanic techniques with elements of Celtic cosmology and spirituality. Investigate shamanic journeys, contact with power animals, working with nature spirits, and shamanic healing in the Celtic context.

Integrating Celtic Ethics into Daily Life: Celtic ethics is not just a set of abstract principles, but a practical guide to living a more ethical, meaningful, and harmonious life. Continue to reflect on Celtic values and integrate them into your daily actions and choices:

Regular Ethical Self-Reflection: Take time to reflect on your actions, choices, and behaviors in light of Celtic ethical principles. Ask yourself if you are living with honor, integrity, respect for nature, courage, wisdom, hospitality, and balance. Identify areas where you can improve and align your actions with your values.

Ethics in Relationships: Apply Celtic ethical principles in your personal, family, professional, and community relationships. Seek honesty, justice, compassion, empathy, and respect in all your interactions.

Environmental Ethics: Live more consciously and sustainably, seeking to reduce your environmental impact, protect nature, and honor the sacredness of planet Earth. Adopt ecological practices in your daily life, support environmental causes, and advocate for the preservation of the environment.

Ethics in Magical Practice: Apply Celtic ethical principles in your ritual and magical practices. Use magic responsibly, respectfully, and with positive intention, seeking your own well-being and the common good. Avoid manipulating, harming, or interfering with the free will of others.

The Celtic Journey is an infinite and transformative path. There is no end point or ultimate destination to be reached, but rather a continuous path of learning, growth, and spiritual evolution. Continue to explore, practice, question, experiment, and connect with the rich tapestry of Celtic Spirituality. Allow the ancient Celtic wisdom to guide you, inspire you, and strengthen you on your personal journey, and may the beauty and magic of the Celtic tradition illuminate your path to a fuller, more authentic life connected to the sacred.

Crossing the portal from knowledge to spiritual experience is an act of courage and surrender. Throughout this journey, you have traveled the paths of Celtic tradition, absorbing its wisdom, rituals, and worldview. But true learning lies not only in the words read or the ceremonies performed, but in the way these teachings shape your essence and your presence in the world. Every step taken from here on will be unique, for no two paths are identical – there is only your trail, built by the fusion of ancestral legacy and your own intuition.

As you move forward, remember that there is no hurry, nor a final destination to be reached. Celtic spirituality is a flow, a perpetual cycle of growth, discovery, and connection. At times, you will find absolute clarity; at others, you will face mystery. Both are equally valuable, as they are part of the process of becoming not just a practitioner of the Celtic tradition, but someone who lives it authentically. Allow yourself to make mistakes, learn, adapt, transform – for that is where the true magic of the journey lies.

And so, as you end this cycle and open yourself to the next, trust in your journey. May the mists of the unknown not be an obstacle, but an invitation to enchantment. May nature be your teacher, may the ancestors be your guides, and may the sacred resonate in every gesture, in every word, in every breath. The path continues, ever expanding, and now it belongs to you.

May the Blessing of the Celtic Gods and Goddesses be always with you.

www.ingramcontent.com/pod-product-compliance
Lightning Source LLC
LaVergne TN
LVHW040052080526
838202LV00045B/3596